INVISIBLE CHILDREN

Invisible Children

*

Who are the real losers
at school?

*

JAMES PYE

Oxford   New York
OXFORD UNIVERSITY PRESS
1988

Oxford University Press, Walton Street, Oxford OX2 6DP

Oxford New York Toronto
Delhi Bombay Calcutta Madras Karachi
Petaling Jaya Singapore Hong Kong Tokyo
Nairobi Dar es Salaam Cape Town
Melbourne Auckland

and associated companies in
Berlin Ibadan

Oxford is a trade mark of Oxford University Press

British Library Cataloguing in Publication Data

Pye, James
Invisible children.
1. Learning by school students.
Psychosocial aspects
I. Title
370.15'23
ISBN 0–19–215958–5

Library of Congress Cataloging in Publication Data
Pye, James
Invisible children/James Pye.
p.   cm.
Bibliography: p.
Includes index.
1. High school students—Great Britain—Case studies.
2. Underachievers—Case studies.   3. Teacher–student relationships–
–Great Britain—Case studies.   4. Motivation in education—Case
studies.   I. Title.
LC4696.G7P93   1988   371.92'6—dc 1988–5324
ISBN 0–19–215958–5

Set by Colset Private Ltd.
Printed in Great Britain
at the University Printing House, Oxford
by David Stanford
Printer to the University

For Susie

Acknowledgements

I wish to thank all the teachers, pupils, and students who helped me. They were generous with their time, and without them this book would never have happened. I would like to thank the School of Education at Reading University for making my research possible. I wish also to thank a number of people for their suggestions, support, or encouragement: Christine Park, Kay Wood, Desmond Vowles, Meg Mallalieu, Jean Devoy, Anne Clarke, Marie Booth, Shirley Nield, Sean Lawlor, Carol Ohlenschlager, John Parker, and Mike Kent. I want also to thank my parents David and Pamela Pye for their interest in this book.

Finally, I wish to thank Susie my wife for her editorial acuity, and her tolerance.

Contents

Introduction

The debate about education is at present predominantly technical. Syllabus, curriculum, profile, continuous assessment, external moderation, opt-out, GCSE, TVEI: such are key words and acronyms, with their promise of impatient change, streamlining, updating, rationalization.

Education, however, cannot be improved by means of technical adjustment alone. At the heart of learning is the relation between learner and teacher; but in the current debate we hear little about it. Ask someone, though, for her good memories of school, and more often than not she will talk of a particular teacher whose enthusiasm and affection were critical; who led her, perhaps, to lasting interest in a subject, or fed her confidence when it was starving.

In a very young child's learning, it is its relationship with its parents which provides optimism, information, safety. A good relationship between teacher and learner in school—and afterwards—is of much the same nature. Just as children are lucky who have generous, grown-up parents, so are pupils and students fortunate who benefit from such 'parental' relationships with their teachers. And it is certain that no technical alterations, nor changes of any kind, can have their intended effect on schools if teachers and pupils cannot know, like, respect, and understand each other in circumstances that encourage them to do so.

Such truths need restating, and they need to be exemplified in new ways. That is one of the central purposes of this book.

PART ONE

An account of my early experience as a teacher;
leading to a sequence of accounts of the schooling
of eight of my witnesses.

Some pupils remembered, others forgotten

I WENT into teaching in 1972, charged with the fervour of the time. I believed that children must be wiser than repressed and alienated adults; and I thought that the transformation of the world would be their responsibility. I would be helping to train their minds for their work. This programme was soon lost in the urgent practicalities of the job, which, after the discipline problems of my first year, I came to find more and more enjoyable.

I enjoyed everything. I don't think I reflected about what I was doing at all. I was too busy; too guilty if I found myself with nothing to do. I taught English—in a small Scottish comprehensive at Glentoul. The ideas fashionable when I trained made it a most seductive subject. I could enthuse about poetry; and my pupils could become poets themselves. 'Express yourselves!' I said—and they did. But the cultural revolution hadn't overwhelmed the old values of Highland education. Academic rigour was felt to be important; and children who further south might have been dismissed as incapable of more than a few CSEs were expected to achieve more. I'd no objection to rigour, and didn't see it as incompatible with self-expression. I enjoyed widening my pupils' vocabularies as much as I enjoyed encouraging them to write poetry. I enjoyed teaching the 'Higher' syllabus, which ordained the understanding and precise use of complex language, almost as much as I enjoyed the wild sessions of improvisation in my drama classes.

I worked hard. What fuelled my labours was partly the comfortable knowledge that what I was doing was useful and politically faultless. The school was comprehensive; many of my pupils were working class. But I was also hungry for my pupils' love. I courted them shamelessly with jokes and enthusiasm and refusal to see anyone as beyond redemption. I saw myself as a sort of saviour: the one the dull could come to for illumination.

Teaching, I was at my best in the role of public speaker stirring up the apathetic and dealing with hecklers—or in the role of a comic warming up an audience or neutralizing a hostile reception. It was a very public act that I revelled in; and my chief concern was to know that I was 'going down well'. Most moves I made were designed for my audience. To walk towards a pupil in a class silently working on a task I had set them, smile at her, say in a warm voice, 'How are you getting on?' was to advertise my warmth, my unauthoritarian friendliness, my concern. And her answering smile and acceptance of my act said to me not so much, 'Thank you, I need your help and welcome it' (though it did say that as well, because I was adept at making myself welcome) but, '*We* love and appreciate you and know that you have our best interests at heart. We think you're great.'

When I was left alone with a pupil—taking one home, for instance, after a drama rehearsal—I often found it difficult to talk to her, when a few minutes before we might have seemed the best of friends.

The relationships I made fed my craving to be liked. I did also develop a 'professional' determination to attend to the needs of each of my pupils. But this aim was far weaker than my craving. The relationships I made were with those who best fed it, rather than with those who were most in need of my parental attention. And each relationship was a banner for all to read: this person is a popular teacher. It wasn't enough to be liked; I had to be seen to be liked.

In this compulsion, I was typical of a certain, and common, sort of teacher. Teaching attracts many immature people—lured to schools and the company of children as if to a time of their own lives where they truly belong. I cannot substantiate this except by saying that whenever I go into a school I sense its corroboration. And many people I have spoken to, who have never been teachers, come away from visits to school staffrooms haunted by a feeling that they have not been in the company of adults. Perhaps the innumerable teachers who *are* adult tend to be inconspicuous; so the visitor remembers those who are not: the superannuated prefects strutting up to notice boards, the prattlers in small noisy groups whose voices and gestures are somehow incestuous, excitable, adolescent. Whenever I go into a staffroom I sense their presence.

The trouble, perhaps, is that most secondary teachers recruit themselves straight from university, before they have had a chance to become adults among adults. Instead they find themselves among children and adolescents again, and their development as human beings may thereafter be in jeopardy. When I was doing my research I did a certain

amount of work with a group of student teachers. Two of them were going to be marvellous teachers; some of the others I thought likely to be competent. But none, except two who had decided to try teaching in their thirties after working in other trades, was adult.

At any rate, I want to assume for the moment that I was not untypical of many 22-year-olds embarking on a teaching career. Wanting to be liked—a desire perhaps shared by all teachers in varying degrees—was certainly a very powerful determinant of my choice of who should receive the great gift of my attention. Here now is an account of several pupils who did.

Hamish

Hamish was Glaswegian and proud of it. He had emigrated to the Highlands to live with his elder sister and her husband when his parents' marriage broke up. He was in the first third-year class I taught. From the start he recognized both my Englishness and my naïvety—and that I was easy meat. He did more or less what he wanted with me. The fact that I often couldn't understand what he was saying did not help. I remember him using words I had never heard. Lessons with his class were chaotic and my attempts to create order ineffectual. One day I shouted at the top of my voice for quiet. Shortly afterwards Hamish began to say, 'Sir! Sir!' in an equally loud voice.

'Yes, Hamish, what is it?'

'Ye've made Shona greet, Sir.'

I recall my confusion so well: not only did I not know what 'greet' meant; but once he had explained to everyone's amusement except mine that it meant cry, I didn't have the confidence to realize that he was provoking me by suggesting that I was the cause of the girl's distress. The just plausible idea was that my shout had been too much for a sensitive girl to bear. Hamish gloated. He had the whole class in no time agreeing that it was shameful for me to have made this girl so unhappy.

I tried to be nice to him; I tried to understand him; I tried to win him to my side.

'For Christ's sake, will ye no shut up an gie's a bit of peace?' he'd say, cards in fist, when I told him to put them away.

'No I won't shut up, because I want you to work, Hamish. What's the point of you being here if you just play cards,' I would say, patiently, endlessly.

When we met in the street or in the corridor, I'd smile at him, joke

with him—and he would show clearly how much he liked me. And when I became a friend of the local social worker, I discovered that he not only liked me, but that I was one of only two teachers of whom he had anything positive to say.

From then on a bargain was sealed. He would go on giving me trouble: I would be endlessly patient. He would be my difficult foster-son, and I would be his all-forgiving father. He would lead the other boys in discontent, and I would show that my tolerance and love were without end. It was a heroic role that I played well; and we both gained. My success with him was a feather in my mortar board: it showed I was gifted at working with the malcontents. To know that such a hard character liked me was very warming.

Hamish sold himself to me by being unavoidably demanding, and I bought willingly. Many others in the class couldn't compete; and I cannot now even remember their faces, let alone their names. *I gave him far more time and attention than I gave to anyone else in that class.*

Mairhi

Mairhi was a contemporary of Hamish's and became another member of my 'family'. She was very pretty, with eyes I still vividly remember, and making her like me did my male pride good. She was also an excellent actress; and by the time I came to know her, I had already began to turn into a drama fanatic. Encouraged by my head of department—without whom I would never have survived my traumatic first year. I joined him in the writing and direction of vast pantomimes. In my first year, we also directed for the music teacher a production of *The Pirates of Penzance*.

I became a slave, spending all my free time on the production. I was a willing slave because, like the pupils involved, I loved the excitement of it all. But I was also compelled by a need for approval: to be seen to be so dedicated would do my reputation much good. I recall one evening after a rehearsal—at least two hours after the end of the school day—sitting alone on the stage, gloating at my virtue, making lanterns out of cardboard. The headmaster, on his way home, chatted to me about the production. I was delighted that he saw and acknowledged my slavery.

In my experience, all schools operate a covert apparatus of approval that thrives on such moments. You build your reputation by making your dedication public to the right people at the right time. Heads and their deputies notice, assess, praise, and chalk up good marks. The

process is infantilizing: it helps to ensure that teachers susceptible to perpetual adolescence don't grow up. And dedication—in keeping with the mythology of teaching as vocation, as martyrdom—can become more important than competence. The dangers are fawning on one side, and gross partiality on the other.

Mairhi shared the lead part—which she was given because she had a beautiful singing voice. I first became friendly with her because she started going out with my foster-son Hamish. I godfathered their match, and supported them in their difficulties. Mairhi's family disapproved of Hamish. I made it clear that I thought love more important than class, and that their affair was a good thing. I gave Hamish jobs backstage, and he began to haunt the production—wherever was Mairhi, he was also.

When it came to the performances, they seemed to be forever at my side, Mairhi made-up, *coiffeured* and in a shimmering dress, and Hamish in jeans, with his long fair hair and his black leather jacket. Other teachers helping out often tried to shoo Hamish away; but I, adoring employer, claimed that he was an indispensable part of my staff, so that he could be near his love.

Thus Mairhi joined my family, and we smiled at each other and had a special understanding. In my second year I wooed her to sing in a short play I wrote with my head of department, in which she was a great success, and by means of which my reputation grew. The following year she was in the second class taking Higher in English, and I taught her. She was sure she would not pass; so I was determined that she should. I took her on as a challenge to my skill, and out of natural loyalty to a member of my 'family'. I set traps of success for her self-denigration. I tripped up her apathy time after time, and fought each new doubt with patience and guile. Teaching Mairhi was one of my first experiences of the pleasure of building confidence.

She passed. *I cannot now remember one other member of her class.*

That is not to say that I wholly neglected them. Part of my act was tireless assiduity. I marked books thoroughly and often, and spent hours preparing good lessons. But how many of her forgotten classmates could have benefited from the extra of my subtle partiality, my dogged insistence that they were capable of a pass? How many of them had a secret conviction of their stupidity that I could have exposed and challenged—as I challenged Mairhi's?

I would encourage her outside class time. She was a member of the Drama Club, and when I was taking her back home after a meeting, in the minibus, she would sit in the front—as publicly proud of being my friend as I was proud of her affection—and ask me how I thought she was doing. I would tell her again and again that she was doing all right, that I had confidence in her, and that she must have the confidence to believe that she would pass. Her mother knew me; and when we met in the street, we would talk about Mairhi's English, and I would repeat my belief that she just needed to trust her ability and all would be well.

I think that both Hamish and Mairhi gained from their dealings with me. Hamish, I suspect, was a self-hater whose life had taught him that he was probably unlovable. Testing me to the limit, he found that I still liked him, and that must have been of psychological benefit. Mairhi gained from my determination that she should succeed—which led me to outwit her lack of confidence.

Robert

It was not just the difficult, or attractive, or academically interesting who lured me. Some of my pupils with learning difficulties I found very interesting.

Apart from the boy himself, what I recall about Robert's class is that it was very large. In Glentoul, classes could sometimes be relatively small—Mairhi's class was about twenty in number (small by whose standards, one might add). But in my second year I taught two classes of over forty for history; and there were more than thirty in Robert's class. I can see him sitting in the desk nearest to mine, at the front of the class. I see my windows, with their view of high mountains and a vast stretch of sky; and beneath the windows a ledge covered in my erratic cardboard-box filing system. All the desks are occupied; but I can recall no other faces.

Putting myself back in that room makes me feel a sense of regret, of loss. The space at the front near the blackboard was my stage for five years; and however I may now try to expose my motives, what went on in that room was energetic and often successful. It is perhaps irrelevant that my devotion was to myself, if all I want to do is the arithmetic of the profits and losses of my work. Undoubtedly, many gained. What Robert gained I am not sure; but he certainly became another member of my 'family'.

He was a short 13-year-old when I knew him. Long hair was still fashionable for boys then, and his was in roughly assembled wedges: a wedge for a fringe, and two larger wedges attached to the sides of his head. It was light brown in colour, framing an intelligent, very lively face. His smile is what I remember best about him: he smiled at everything and everyone.

He talked very fast and incoherently, becoming quickly excited, especially if he were talking about animals, about which he was extremely knowledgeable. He wrote at speed too, and at length; but what he wrote was inscrutable. Jargon faltered trying to define him. Was he dyslexic? We thought not, not really knowing what the word meant. As a compromise, I told his mother that the best way of describing his difficulties was to say that he was word-blind. But words he certainly wrote, confidently and rapidly, forceful purpose accelerating them from line to line, until at the end of a two-page piece, they would look like wire, vaguely indented and looped.

I began with what he wrote, taking from it the few words that were recognizable, re-forming them in small lists, and asking him to learn them. I made sensible families of such words—assembling, say, five or six all ending in 'ion'. Dedicated and eager, and intelligent—I was never in any doubt that he was highly intelligent—he would take on trust anything I asked him to do, and work hard at it.

For a day or two he would retain the shape of certain words, and the principles that linked others into families. Then the slate of his memory would be wiped clean. I'd ask him to write one of the words he had tried to learn. He would fail, and would smile his most skilful smile: of self-deprecation and apology.

I sat him at the desk in front of me, and taught him on his own, bringing him into the whole class again for public occasions like discussions. I became in a way obsessed by his difficulties, because they seemed so unreasonable. Why should someone of such obvious intelligence be so impeded?

We gave him all that we could in the English Department: extra remedial help; sessions with various experts, who were as baffled as we were. He liked my attention, and he liked me, and he worked hard to help himself—but all to no evident purpose.

Like Mairhi, he challenged my skill; but my skill was useless. I liked Robert enormously, and became his advocate, his sponsor. His life was made difficult by his academic oddity. He was labelled 'thick' by his classmates, though he was far from unpopular. But even their liking could hurt him, because it could make them tolerant and patronizing: he didn't want to be a mascot. So I would try hard to make my respect for his intelligence as obvious as I could. Sometimes in discussions he would come up with ingenious, odd ideas—all signalled by frantic waving of his arms to draw attention to the fact that he had something to say. I was vigilant for such chances to praise his originality, to make public the fact that I valued him, and to counter those who thought him stupid.

My relationship with Robert had obvious advantages for my reputation, too. I was the one who had the acuity to see through misconceptions of his ability to the intelligent person beneath. I was the teacher who, even though burdened by drama rehearsals and exams and books to mark, found the time to give Robert extra teaching, and to devise special exercises to train his memory. And it flattered my image of myself—as being someone who treated all even-handedly and saw talent and intelligence in the most unlikely people—to be seen spending so much time with him, poring over his work, smiling my encouragement.

But, again, what interests me now is to realize that I remember no other child in Robert's class, and to ask myself what proportion of my time I must have spent with him. Important, too, is that like Hamish and Mairhi he was unusual and interesting. Hamish was unusually aggressive, and unusually fond of me; Mairhi was unusually beautiful, with an unusual voice. And the contradiction between Robert's intelligence and his performance was certainly unusual. *There was nothing ordinary or invisible or unremarkable about him.*

Shona

Shona was the sort of pupil a teacher who loves his subject longs to teach. She loved literature, revelled in it, wrote precisely and elegantly about it; smiled her appreciation secretly and seductively of particular lines, words—epiphanies. She was in a top fifth-year class I taught in my last year at Glentoul. Like Robert, she sat at the front of the class. I thought her beautiful, though some would have disagreed, she most of all. Her elder sister was more conventionally attractive, with pretty, neat features and a slender figure. But Shona had such large brown eyes—which she hid most of the time behind a fringe; and an astounding smile that she only very rarely allowed to be seen.

Her demeanour was cautious, apologetic, diffident. In class she would only speak if asked—if pressed; so our conversations took place on paper; and aloud on the frequent occasions I contrived before and after lessons, or during them when everyone was working, but not so quietly that she would have been easily heard. She would write superb essays—which made me suspect that I must be an excellent teacher—and I would write an equally superb essay in red beneath, elaborating and amplifying her thoughts.

She walked with a slight stoop of deprecation; and I thought, glibly, that I knew her story. 'She thinks she's ugly, because her sister's so pretty and socially accomplished, and she thinks her mouth is too big, and that she's overweight. But I will make her realize how gifted and beautiful she is.' That was my phantasy, and not a particularly meretricious one.

I tried to make Shona feel special. I would spend longer poring over her book in class than anyone else's. I would smile at her a lot, and always say hello, which would make her blush. When necessary I wrote long eulogistic reports. When her parents came to a meeting with teachers, I told them how gifted I thought their daughter was. When her class wrote essays and I took the pile home with me, it was to her book that I turned first, or last, saving it up to encourage me after the rest.

I do not think a lesson passed without my making contact with her in some way: addressing a remark directly to her; engaging her in discreet conversation; explaining something I had written in her book. Again, *I cannot now recall another member of her class.*

Only the remarkable

I could have picked other remarkable pupils with whom I made close relationships. Others I do remember were, like Hamish, Mairhi, Robert and Shona, either the academically successful, or interesting poets or actors, or beautiful, or very difficult to manage.

They all gave me as much as I gave them, or more; and they all had something that distinguished them from their contemporaries. They attracted first my attention and then my dedication.

I should not criticize myself too severely for what I gave them, nor for the fact that I gave them—with 'subtle partiality'—so much. They gained, as did all who joined my 'family'. Even though my own greed to be liked may have been outlandish, what my example does suggest is probably true of all teachers: that what makes them allocate their time and attention are not just 'professional' aims such as the impartial desire to give all their due, but also murkier promptings to do with their own needs.

What of the rest? What of those who had lost confidence and who worked hard to elude my attention? What of them, most of all?

Quiet elusive pupils I do recall

It is seven years since I left Glentoul. During that time, memories of
pupils have grown dimmer and dimmer; but it is as if I had been teaching
the four I have just described yesterday. That I recall them so well is a
measure of the complexity of my relationships with them, and of the
pleasure they gave me.

I have scoured my mind for memories of the 'invisible' nice—the sort
of pupils with whom this book is greatly concerned. But they seem all to
have merged into one pleasant, composite girl. No, I see one now, as I
write, though I cannot remember her name. She blushed easily—I do
remember that; and she came to school one day with a new haircut that
caused her endless, undesired, and embarrassing prominence. I see a
great bold wave breaking on a forehead; but I am not sure that the
features I sense beneath the wave are hers, or from a vague collage made
up of hundreds like her.

I do recall two pupils who did their best to elude me; but only because
they eventually forced themselves on my attention. I can't remember the
name of the first, but I do remember her face. Her habitual expression
was of reserve. She neither smiled much nor frowned; looked neither
happy nor sad. She looked cautious, uncommitted, distant. I am pretty
sure that I taught her in my first year at Glentoul, when she was in the
second year, but I recall nothing about her work. My memory of that
class is dominated by two very clever boys, and two girls who became
later my most loyal actresses. This girl—let's call her Catherine—was
neither clever nor stupid; and I would lay money on her having been
a studious underliner of dates and titles: twice, neatly with a ruler, in
blue ink.

I think I next taught her in the fourth year, but I may have taught her
in the year between. She was by then in a low stream, officially taking O
level as an incentive and pious hope—though everyone knew that few in
the class would pass. I did get to know Catherine a little better that year,
through her dutiful, neatly written work. She was the best at English in
the class; and I thought she might get a C.

I gave her the attention her work required and deserved; and she gave
me in return—more work. No smiles, friendship, or flattering revelation of her personality—nothing that made me feel liked. Such
inattention to my needs always made me feel slight resentment. I craved
to be liked; but all she gave me was more dull, dutiful work.

My attention was monopolized by four rowdy boys. I kept them in order with tact and guile and insistence on plenty of work. They were taxing. I needed to show that I liked them—which I did—or I would have been lost; and the effort they required of me left little time for Catherine, quietly working away.

I judged the quality of her work against the rest and so ventured to hope for a C. But I think it was her demeanour, her face, and her neat writing that suggested this grade; and, of course, the predetermined expectation that anyone placed in her stream could at best only achieve such a result.

So it was a jolt when she was awarded an A.

My reactions were mixed. First, I was pleased for the feather in my cap of having taught an F stream pupil to get an A pass. I was also surprised, and began for the first time to think about Catherine. But I had no chance to turn thought into action. She was leaving school. Our interest in her had not been necessary for her to win the modest success of a few decent O levels—she gained two other good passes. If we had taken notice of her, perhaps we would have discovered someone for whom *more* education was appropriate, and perhaps she would have stayed on. Our ignorance of her may have ended her education for good. Had we known and related to her, her education, at any rate, might have become active and exciting, rather than automatous and dull and dutiful.

I remember Catherine only because she did something unexpected, out of character: she became remarkable, like Hamish, Mairhi, and the others.

Alasdair

I recall this boy because I tried to fathom him, tried to be liked by him, and failed. Even though he was so obstinately elusive, it was impossible not to be attracted to him. He was not ordinary. I knew Catherine so little, that I never bothered to ask myself or any of her other teachers any questions about her. I never talked to anyone else about her. I did not talk about Alasdair either.

I did not teach him until the third year, by which time he was in the same stream as Catherine had been, with similar expectations pinned to him. But in his first two years, though I hadn't taught him, he had been in a large group I had taken for 'extra-curricular drama'. I came to know him as someone who didn't like being asked to talk; who seemed peripheral, reluctant to take part. But when he was asked to mime, he did so with precision, almost with brilliance.

He was small and dark, with very large eyes, and a wary, alert expression. Teaching him, I began with the presupposition that he was bright, despite his low stream. There'd been something vivid about his mime's precision that suggested equivalently vivid intelligence. Asked with two others to pick up an imaginary piano, it would be Alasdair who'd create a fat piano leg before my eyes, with delicate suggestions of his hands; and Alasdair whose posture best spoke heaviness, the controlled alarm it is impossible not to feel, carrying something so daunting. His mime made my interest inevitable.

In class he sat next to Ralph who, in physique and personality, could not have been more different: he was round, ebullient, witty, anarchic. They amused each other—and Ralph could never control his laughter. But I would only ever see Alasdair smile. Occasionally they would come into my room together, in the middle of amusement; but just as when in class I looked in their direction to see Alasdair smiling, his face would quickly compose itself, so when he crossed the classroom threshold, he became cautious and inscrutable.

He was inscrutable on approach, as well. He would give nothing away. His rebuff was tantalizing. He would, as I spoke, lift his eyes very briefly; but they would dip down and away from mine almost before I had seen them, but not quite. So I was able to intercept a look alert and understanding, a look of instant shrewd surveillance. It was like being understood and refused by a shy animal.

If I said I liked what he had written, I might get another look, just as brief, to which had been added a scruple of pleasure. It was as if he were saying to himself, 'I'd better be a little bit more forthcoming: that's what you are supposed to do when people are nice to you.'

His writing was as evasive as his demeanour. For a start, his letters were cramped and small—his handwriting itself seemed to be trying to hide. In routine comprehension exercises, he would write fairly clear though not very well-spelt answers. On a poor day, his answers—inaccurate and almost illegible—would yawn their boredom. Sometimes the stories and essays he wrote would be of like quality; but sometimes parts of them might attain the vividness of his miming.

I would acknowledge the good stuff and ask for more of it. I'd use all my skill to exhort and persuade and chivvy—to make contact. But it was no good. His work was not important to him. It meant nothing. Then I noticed that he amused Ralph by drawing cartoons. I persuaded Alasdair to show them to me. They were strip cartoons featuring characters of his own invention. One series took place in a neatly suggested Wild West; another was Scottish and depended on tartan shibboleths wittily handled. In their bubbles, his characters spoke more tidily and fluently than he ever wrote any of his work for me—even when I told him to do an exercise again.

His cartoons were impressive. I told him that he could do some more in class, as a reward if his work were good enough. But I soon realized that this tactic was a loser. It was to ask him to bring something from his own private, pleasurable world into the world of my lessons—which he found uninteresting, and which he survived by denying that they were happening at all. Compliantly, he did draw some cartoons for me; but without conviction, almost with embarrassment. They were not as good as the ones he did for Ralph.

I persevered. I bullied him into letting me have copies of some of his 'private' work, and put them on the wall as proof of his skill and intelligence. I was sure that if I could only make him believe in my lessons, his work would become as convincing as his mime. But he eluded me.

In my fervour I began to feel disgruntled. I began to ignore him—as he wanted—and to accept what was probably his own low opinion of his academic ability. I went on being friendly to him, and marking his work; but I gave up trying to reach him—trying to make him one of my 'family'. I had invited him, and he had declined.

I remember, late that winter, going for a walk with a friend beside a loch near Alasdair's home territory. He lived in a small cottage down a side road—some six miles from the main road, and twenty-five miles from the school. In order to catch the school bus in the morning, he had to be up at half-past six.

His house was on the estate for which his father worked. It stood in a group of three or four others, with the loch on one side and a steep mountain on the other. We came on him quite suddenly, in a clearing in the birches near the house. He was chopping wood, and had paused to watch a squirrel.

He saw us, looked round, and smiled. I felt somehow that we were trespassing, so I just said hello, and we walked on. His smile had been open, unconstrained—almost triumphant; aggressive, as if he were saying, 'This is what is real, this is where I belong, and your caper at school is just a sham—' I took his smile as proof that he would always elude me.

Acknowledgement

I believe that the forming of a 'family' should be seen as psychologically inevitable. Teachers *cannot* connect closely to all their pupils; but they need, in the presence of so much humanity, to be close to some of it. Those who benefit can do so enormously; just as the rewards for the teacher can be great.

The rewards I sought say a great deal about my own particular needs, though I have argued that they were not unique. And every teacher needs to be liked and appreciated. Many people I have interviewed about their school careers have provided me with illuminating accounts of the crucial effect on them of a relationship with a particular teacher. In each case, what is described is a relationship with someone who valued and *acknowledged* them.

I use this word to mean that a teacher treats a pupil as an interesting and unpredictable individual, not as an inhabitant of a convenient generality. Pupils will gain from teachers with whom they make close relationships, time, patience and regard. But most important of all, they will gain from being acknowledged as *not* wholly known, as able to surprise.

Pupils who are abandoned to generalities will gain from a conscientious teacher a certain amount of attention, red ink on their books, 'professional' interest. But such abandonment ends doubt; and it is doubt that allows for the possibility of surprise.

I neither knew nor acknowledged Catherine. She was in a class that I had already decided, before beginning to teach it, would never produce more than a C pass; and I decided after teaching her that she might achieve a C pass if she were lucky. About that judgement I had no doubt. I took her for a known quantity who would never surprise. I tried to acknowledge Alasdair; but he wanted none of me. After I had made up my mind that he *was* limited, I gave up hoping for surprise—gave up seeing him as unpredictable.

The danger of not being acknowledged—of the decision that you will definitely and always be capable of a C rather than an A—is that the expectation will *create* the predicted result. Labelling theory has taught us about this process. If you are firmly seen as a C, it will be hard to believe yourself an A. (It is probably no accident that Catherine reserved her final surprise for the exam—over which I had no control, and in which she was free of my expectations. Perhaps it was liberating to her to know that I would not be marking her papers.)

But acknowledgement brings with it the hope of surprise—the expectation of delight, of amazement. When Mairhi wrote an essay which corroborated my faith in her, the delight I felt was the delight I had hoped for all the time I'd been teaching her. It was an inevitable pleasure at something good written by a pupil I greatly liked. She wrote an elegant satire on the predicament of the examinee, by imagining herself sitting an examination in which she was asked to write an essay about sitting an examination. There was nothing particularly original about her idea; but her treatment was apt, adept and concise. It was her own intelligence she doubted; and I could flourish refutation of her doubt in her face—with delight.

This last word interests me. Perhaps by 'acknowledgement' I am talking about a relationship like that between a parent and a young child—in which a teacher is truly *in loco parentis,* and is *delighted* by his child and his child's progress.

Adolescence as hypothesis

What interests me most about Alasdair was that I did not—nor was I expected to—talk to any of my colleagues about him, except casually. What I now think should have happened, is that we should have united to try to crack his enigma; should have surrounded him, guilefully, with our interest and affection; should at least have shared our suspicions about his gifts. Perhaps we would have decided that we should not take his uninterested work as valid evidence of his ability. (I do at least know that his performance in other subjects was similar to his performance in mine.) Had we talked and thought, perhaps we would have agreed on a common approach to him, with powerful unanimity; and I might, at any rate, have realized that my own revision of early high expectations was prompted by disgruntlement and rejection.

Let us suppose, for the sake of argument, that fear and self-dislike forced him into concealment and mediocrity; that a sort of weakness stifled his gifts. What I and his other teachers did, was to accept what he showed of himself—governed by that weakness—as his whole story.

Many would argue that school thus accurately reflects life, where the strong succeed. This is a Social Darwinist notion that I find indigestible. It says that the weakest should be allowed to go to the wall, because they are going to end up there anyway. But I think it is a necessary precaution to argue that in adolescence we *are* not quiet, or assertive, or shy, or even bright. *We are trying out the hypothesis that we are.*

Demeanour in adolescence should not be seen as the expression of established personality; nor should performance educationally be seen as the expression of established gifts: both should be seen as experiment to test hypothesis.

If a theory (I use this word interchangeably with 'hypothesis') is a meagre one—I'm shy, I'm hopeless, I'm average, people don't take an interest in me because I am dull and uninteresting—school should offer circumstances and approaches which allow alternative theories to be tried out.

When I was talking to the staff of the comprehensive school where I did much of my research, an interesting discussion of this issue took place. I met strong opposition to the notion that those who speak little in class or not at all—those who avoid prominence—should not only be encouraged to do so, but *trained* to do so as well. I had quoted the words of a girl I had interviewed about her school career, who said sadly, 'If only someone had told me how to ask a question—I didn't know how.'

'But they are shy, quiet people who don't *want* to join in! They blush and look uncomfortable and make me feel cruel if I persist,' was the argument. 'They don't want to join in, so it's kinder to leave them. That's the sort of people they are . . .'

My argument was that it might be school that had trained them to keep silent and to blush; so school should offer training in an alternative demeanour. Then an ally came to my rescue. I had already interviewed her about her own school career. Now a teacher herself, she had found my work interesting, and said that she thought she herself had been an 'invisible' pupil.

'No!' she said. 'It just isn't true that they are the sort of people who want to be left alone, that they want to keep silent and never ask questions. They want to join in but they can't. They want to be a different sort of person altogether.'

Then she used what has seemed ever since a most potent analogy: 'They want to join in but they can't—just as I can't bear to pull off a large piece of sticking plaster quickly myself: I need someone else to do it.'

In other words, we sometimes need—especially in adolescence—other people to help rip off our old, weary, unhelpful, but adhesive theories of ourselves.

CHAPTER TWO

David: lost pupil acknowledged

I AM not sure why I decided to give up being a teacher in comprehensive schools. I think that I did begin to see—though dimly—that at the age of 28, at the end of my time at Glentoul, I hadn't really grown up; but that's another story.

I left. Before I did, I was short-listed for the job of head of department at another similar school. With a week to go before the interviews, I chickened out. I just couldn't see myself as someone taking his first judicious step up the upholstered ladder to headmasterhood. Dimly I sensed egg stains on my personality.

Not long afterwards, I found myself in the city. I wrote a murky novel. The first agent I sent it to sensibly declined to promote it for me. I ran out of money, and took a temporary job teaching English again, in a huge comprehensive. I taught there successfully for the best part of a year, and toyed with the idea of staying: a permanent job was available.

If I try to recall my pupils there in the same way that I have tried to recall my Scottish pupils, I come up with the same mixture of vivid memory and fog. My fifth-year class for instance: I can picture the room in which I taught them; and I can see the shape made in the room by a class of a little over twenty pupils. I can put features on five faces; and of those five, one laughs at me as if I'd been teaching her last week.

Sonia was wonderful. She had so many voices, for a start: she could speak faultless middle-class English, with appropriate deportment, and could *be* the person who spoke and held herself thus for days. She could also speak Cockney, and Glaswegian, and in a voice that was neither of these two. She performed for me the same service as Hamish did in Scotland. She had the reputation of being very difficult indeed; but I got on with her from the outset, and my success became generally known, and helped to make my reputation.

She could be alarming. I remember teaching another class, and Sonia bursting in, running to my desk and draping herself all over it, head held elegantly on a hand propped by an elbow, to laugh at me and say critical things about my appearance. Another time I was walking soberly to the secretary's office, when Sonia ran up, grabbed my arm, waltzed with me into the office, and announced to several onlookers that this was Jim, her fiancé, and we were just off to choose the curtains for our new home.

I recall four others; two disruptive but luckily often absent, and two whose work was very good. The rest have all faded.

But I was greedy for change, for novelty; and so I applied for and was appointed to a job teaching in the adolescent ward of a psychiatric hospital. This ward was housed in a low modern building with lawn on one side and trees on the other. I was attracted by its smallness. The ward had about twenty beds; and in school at any one time there were unlikely to be more than twelve pupils. Much of the work, I was told on my first visit, was on a one-to-one basis.

I took with me to this job my experience as a teacher in a very different setting; and the insight I began to acquire into what I had been doing was partly the result of the great contrast between that setting and my new circumstances. My equipment as a teacher soon proved itself faulty, because I could not operate in my accustomed way. But to begin with the novelty was so great that I did not have time to consider my inadequacies.

I remember my first staff meeting at the Ashby Unit. The senior registrar listed patients' symptoms for me so that I knew what to expect. One girl had a hysterically paralysed hand that had been clenched so long that its palm was a 'bit messy'; another girl, whose distressed mewing we could hear from the meeting room as she wandered up and down the corridor outside, was 'floridly psychotic'—my first encounter with that phrase. A boy hadn't spoken for a month. There were three entrenched anorexics, one of whom discreetly vomited most food she was given, managing to evade nurses' vigilance in order to do so. Another of the starvers was so severe a case that she might well be dead within the next five years, he told me.

David's legs were hysterically paralysed. Why, I asked. Though terrified by the menu so far, I was still curious. The registrar shrugged his shoulders. No one really knew, though there were theories.

My fear was unnecessary. Even the three patients who were psychotic ceased to alarm after a day or two, though they monopolized my attention. Having them in school was an unpredictable but enjoyable business. An hour's lucid school work might be followed by improbable demands. I want to bake a green cake. Tomorrow, cooking's tomorrow. No, now. We're going to do some history now, I'd insist, having been told that structure could reassure and be therapeutically useful for even the most elaborately florid. Tears might follow, or assent. It was impossible, often, to predict which.

It is important to note, from the start, that my experience equipped me to look for pupils who would reward me most—who were attractive and interesting. My source of reward, of 'job satisfaction', had been relationships with some pupils, and the comforting exchange of my interest and enthusiasm for their affection. So it was the psychotics who first attracted me, and with whom I made the equivalent of relationships. My dealings with them were not as essentially satisfying as with pupils like Shona and Hamish and Mairhi; but novelty and unpredictability went far to compensate.

From the very beginning, I was dividing my time and my attention unequally. And I was never, at any one moment, dealing with more than five pupils at a time.

The anorexics interested me too—again for novelty and unpredictability. They would come in emaciated and be put straight to bed. Privileges were at this stage removed, to be restored gradually as reward for weight gained. A radio would be returned, for instance, and eventually a girl would be allowed to get up. A drop in weight, however, would mean a return to bed.

Samantha was charming, intelligent, and icy. She was near enough her 'target weight' to be up and in school, where she spent as much time as she was allowed cooking. Like many anorexics, she was a very good cook, though she never tasted anything she made. I liked sparring with Samantha. She was taking English O level. She would write me an essay.

'You have a large vocabulary and you write with fluency,' I'd tell her, 'but there's nothing of you in this, is there?' But there was no chance of a crack in her suave surface.

'Yes, I know,' she'd say. 'It's awfully tedious, isn't it?'

She implied that it wasn't really her work at all. She had occasionally to make a sortie into the world to placate people like me with whatever seemed appropriate—an English essay, a nice smile. She knew what people wanted; and if they didn't like what she gave them, she'd probably find something more suitable next time. There was nothing to worry about, because none of their ploys and their frowns could distract her from her job, which was to kill herself slowly and politely.

She was certainly 'entrenched'. She made me and all of us feel sad, affectionate, helpless.

But I missed my adoring audiences—whole classes I'd trained to laugh at every joke, with front rows of pretty girls who would return every smile and work assiduously just to please me. And many I was now given to teach were very dull. It so happened that there was a majority of the depressed and neurotic when I first went to work at the Ashby; and they were too preoccupied to notice me much, far less appreciate me. Like Samantha, most did the work they were set; but dully and diligently.

It was no use acting. There weren't enough to form a good audience; and without a few more of them, how could I stride and posture and joke? I nearly became an actor—I spent much of my time at university acting—and only rejected such a career because I thought, with puritanical disdain fashionable in the late sixties and early seventies, that acting was indulgent and politically incorrect. But of course, as a teacher, I'd acted all the time.

So I felt split—between boredom and extreme interest in the psychotics and anorexics. If only they were all mad, I thought.

I recall two of the depressed in particular. Pat was tiny, and never looked me in the eye. She'd been referred for depression, and still seemed very depressed. I would walk to her desk, and her small-featured face would duck behind hair. I would ask her to show me the work she'd done—an exercise in English comprehension, let's say. She would produce from beneath her desk a small, timid, white hand and gently touch her book, in a gesture so self-deprecating and reluctant it was difficult to persist and look at what she had written. Her manner clearly suggested that to notice her at all was a sort of violence; and to look at something she had committed to paper more violent still. Whatever she wrote would be competent; but if I praised her, she would try to make herself invisible, flinching into herself slowly and discreetly. As yet I was unskilled in dealing with someone so withdrawn; she made me feel cruel for noticing her, so I gave her a minimum of attention, which was just what she wanted but not what she needed. However, with so few to attend to, I could not fail to spend a certain amount of time with her.

David I remember far better, because he was the true beginning of my research for this book.

David

David's legs were hysterically paralysed. When I arrived, he was spending half his day on crutches, and half with a walking-frame. When he needed to get somewhere fast, he was allowed a wheelchair. His legs behaved like dead appendages—and looked as limp and ruined as did my leg when I was run over and broke my thigh-bone. His feet looked shapeless, as if his shoes had been stuffed like a dummy's.

He too was a good head-ducker. I can see him now in the classroom, sitting at one of the eight desks, his head bowed, his face expressionless. He was of medium height, with longish, thick hair cut with a low fringe like a helmet, beneath which his eyes could skulk. Then, his face looked stupid and unalluring.

I would give him work to do—history and English, in which his school had entered him for CSE—and he would sit in silence doing it, covering paper slowly in his minuscule handwriting. When I looked at his work, he would duck, and whisper an answer to any question I asked, never looking up at me.

Sitting with him was depressing. His blankness could douse my optimism easily. A smile or any welcome would cause a movement of his mouth so discreet as to be barely decipherable. A question would be answered monosyllabically, after a pause so deep my spirits had fallen into it.

I didn't dislike him. I both liked and felt sorry for him; but as his company was dull I did not seek it. He was physically disturbing, too. His legs looked dead, and his hands, shoulders and back seemed to lapse and droop in sympathy.

As for his abilities, I assumed that David was in all ways what he seemed to be: an unimaginative, not very intelligent boy, who might pass four or five CSEs moderately well. I would give him his work, let him do it, read and mark it, and give it back with a minimum of discussion.

Now, David and Pat were the equivalent at the Ashby of all those children I knew in comprehensives and now find most difficult to recall: those for whom I cannot provide a single feature, a single memory. Looking at lists of names for classes I taught in my first two jobs, I recall a few people vividly—such as those I described in my last chapter; several other names summon vague, loose memories that do not quite turn into faces, personalities, occasions; and several others still, mean nothing at all.

Had I taught David in Scotland—before he lost the use of his legs— his name would soon have come to mean nothing at all. Why I now propose to go into the details of David's startling story is that it exemplifies, in an extreme way, what can happen when a pupil becomes anonymous; disappears; is unacknowledged, and abandoned to absurdly insufficient theories about his nature and abilities.

David's story

Five years after first meeting him, I interviewed David. I wanted to know, from his point of view, what had happened before his admission to the Ashby Unit. I wanted especially to know what had been happening to him in school; and what his experience of school education had been like.

It became clear that he had worked hard and for a long time before his breakdown, to disappear and present himself as uninteresting. Paralysis was a final stage of a process which had been taking him further and further away from the world outside his home; which, to all intents and purposes, was school.

In the third year at his secondary modern school he missed a lot of time from illness. In his fourth year—shortly before his breakdown—he missed most of the spring term, with migraines, mysterious vomiting, visits to hospital for tests to find out what was wrong.

Meanwhile he stayed at home.

The boundaries of the house were a shell. I didn't go out, I didn't have to go out, I wasn't expected to go out. I wasn't expected to meet anybody; I wasn't expected to interact with anybody. And there was no—expectation of me. I was left here in complete—isolation . . .

I interviewed him at his home—a neat house towards the end of a street in a small village, with open fields behind and in front.

He disappeared, then, into his 'shell'. But intrusive people kept testing him, trying to find out what was wrong. A doctor, in May, said he couldn't find anything wrong, and he didn't know what to do. There was the possibility of David having to go back to school; but the solution to that problem had been slowly evolving for some time by then.

In February after I came out of hospital [for more tests] I started to walk very slowly. It just gradually went from there.

And then—[when he had lost the use of his legs altogether—and here his voice rose, in retrospective triumph] I could not get to school! There was no way I could get there! Which was a—relief.

He added:

I didn't have to find excuses not to go. I used to have to think, now what can I do this time not to go?

It was almost like shutting down. You were just a body in a corner, and just—I don't know—a total withdrawal from everything. You weren't in anything. Your mind wouldn't function.

He had reached a state of perfect inactivity: a state the perpetuation of which was guaranteed by the loss of the use of his legs.

If one thing above all made this state desirable, it was his fear of school. He loathed school and wanted to escape from it for good. He had never liked school, and had always worked hard to make himself as unobtrusive as possible there. It was as if his paralysis was to take to a logical extreme what he had already been trying to do for years. He recalls that in the top class at primary school:

I used to sit in the middle of the room, with my chair backed on to her [the teacher], so I didn't have to catch her eye.

Contact with teachers was kept to a minimum, for fear of treatment such as he received from the headmistress of the primary school, who taught maths:

I think that's one reason why I hate maths so much—she used to put on the bottom of your book, 'see me'—you used to go up there, up to her desk, and she used to shout at you for not understanding . . .

So he learned to avoid, evade:

I used to do perhaps a sum or two and hang it out as long as possible.

He failed the eleven-plus, an exam he knew very little about at his primary school, where the headmistress, he said, chose very early on those who were going to pass, and tutored them assiduously. She let the rest fail, because they were bound to anyway. David claims he knew nothing in detail about the sort of exam the eleven-plus was; and that he had only a vague notion that he was going to have to take it.

So he went to a boys' secondary modern, now a comprehensive. This school was so much larger than his small village primary, and he felt from the start overwhelmed and terrified. He never felt safe there, however hard he worked at his camouflage.

This must have been exhausting to maintain. He never spoke unless forced to, never asked or voluntarily answered questions in class, never raised his eyes in case they might be caught by the marauding gaze of a teacher. I suspect that all his intelligence and imagination were spent on this escapology and concealment. Successfully, to judge by the vagueness of his teachers' comments about him when we contacted them from the Ashby to find out about his work. It was as if they did not really know who we were talking about.

One of the most important of his many tactics was to keep his work mediocre and unremarkable:

If you were average, you weren't embarrassing the teachers, or anything—

Sometimes he would let himself down. In history, his teacher:

would occasionally say, oh this is good, and I used to hate it. I got to the stage when I hated it if I'd done well—everybody used to say, Creep, creep, creep!

He put on the bottom of an essay, 'see me', so like a fool I went and saw him—and he said, I'd just like to tell you this was very good. I was wishing the ground would open up and swallow me there and then.

So by the time I came to teach him, he had been learning camouflage and evasion for years. He had convinced his teachers that his abilities were unremarkable—even in history he was only expected to pass CSE—and he had managed to avoid any of his teachers taking an interest in him. He had, above all, avoided acknowledgement.

And I reacted to him in the same way as his other teachers, as I would have done had I met him in a comprehensive classroom: without much interest, and with less attention.

His devious unconscious supplied hysterical paralysis as a final means of withdrawal. But the irony of this device was that it was bound in the end to make him noticeable. Perhaps it expressed a hidden ambiguity about his predicament; perhaps it was a plea to be rescued as well as an attempt to drown.

Even at the Ashby, though, he managed to make us take too little notice of him. There was a long phase at the beginning of his time there, when we were all allowing ourselves to be persuaded by his unresponsiveness not to respond; by his inaudible voice not to listen when he did in the end speak; by his chameleon evasions not to look closely at him, not even to see him.

He, of course, felt frighteningly exposed after the seclusion of home. Perhaps, as a result, all his old escapologist's skills were working with urgent brilliance during this phase of his time in hospital. The threat was so severe, he had to work desperately hard.

Oh it was terrifying—so many people I didn't know—I wanted to get away. It was really quite frightening—I just didn't know them and I was going to have to spend hours at a time—well, all day, in a completely new environment, full of new people! It was really a threat.

But he couldn't avoid us for ever. Our procedure was to review every patient regularly: to give ourselves frequent opportunities to rethink our approach to them, and to analyse our transactions with them. We were vigilant to find and defeat manipulation and collusion. David had been manipulating us into taking too little notice of him; and we had been colluding with him.

I do not recall the exact sequence of events that led to a radical change in our approach to him. But I do know that it began with a general expression of frustration at a long staff meeting, at which doctors, psychologists, social workers, nurses, and teachers all agreed that they—we—felt resentful that nothing was happening. We prided ourselves on our speedy resolutions of the most intractable problems, but David's legs were still paralysed.

It became clear how angry his resistance was making us. Thinking about the nature of that resistance, we decided that it was above all angry, and implacably hostile to us. It was as if, for the first time, we recognized David's strength and resourcefulness; and we decided to announce our own strength to him, and put our own resourcefulness to work.

We realized, for instance, that for someone *never* to raise his eyes when he was addressed was, if you looked at it from one point of view, evidence of pathological timidity; but looking afresh we could see it also as an expression of dour, obstinate strength; of a refusal to live so powerful that we must steel ourselves to fight it.

This meeting excited me greatly. Such unanimous revision of preconceptions about a not very noticeable pupil is not likely to happen in schools. The power of our unanimity was invigorating. But when I was trying to winkle Alasdair out of his withdrawal, I was working alone.

David begins to appear

No specific strategy was devised when we rallied to his cause. We decided that we must expect far more of him; and stop treating him like an invalid. We decided to provoke change.

Such an idea, was new to me, because as a teacher I had learned to avoid unnecessary provocation of my pupils; and if one of them was peaceful and biddable, it often made sense to leave him alone: he was an ally.

David's wheelchair—which he had been able to use for large parts of the day—was forbidden. Instead, he had to depend entirely on his crutches and his walking-frame. If a journey was a hundred yards down a corridor, he was left to make it on his own; and he was told that at breakfast time, for instance, he must be up early enough to get to the table on time.

He seemed suddenly to become much more visible. He was to be seen everywhere, getting nowhere. But the next time you passed, he would be a couple of feet further on. Jokes became popular, so I'd find myself saying as I passed, 'Slow down a bit, mate!' or something equally provocative.

Tactics bred tactics. 'Let's time his journeys', suggested Stephen, the psychologist. One day, David cut ten minutes off his journey down the long corridor from the dormitory to the dining room—and all day people told him what a great achievement that was. Next day he retracted, and took longer than ever before.

I began to find things to praise in his work. He was taking CSE history, and was studying the Industrial Revolution. He wrote an essay which showed that he knew a great deal about the canal boom. I remember praising him for the extent of his knowledge. Praise made him flinch and try to disappear into his seat. I wanted to go away when he reacted like that, because he made me feel that my attention was cruel. But instead, in the spirit of the new dispensation, I told him what he was doing, and what it made me feel.

'I'm telling you how good your work is and you make me feel as if I'm trying to murder you!'

'Yes.' His assent was deferential, very quiet.

'What d'you mean "yes"? Yes what?' I made a joke of his wanting so little to be singled out for appreciation.

'Your work is good,' I said, in the manner of a martinet accusing a pupil of some crime. 'You know a great deal about this subject!'

'You know far too much,' said Alan, teaching in the same room and always ready to back me up when he thought I was pursuing a useful line. 'In fact this is a disgustingly good essay. Don't do such a good one again.'

'Or we'll expect more of the same, and then where will you be?'

Working in such close harmony with another teacher was yet another novelty. I learnt a great deal from Alan, who was more experienced than I was; and I learnt especially about the power of working with someone else rather than alone, as one tends to work in schools.

When David began to laugh—however discreetly—at such sallies, we began to feel that we were getting somewhere. He says that at this stage he did begin tentatively to enjoy some of the new contact he was having with people; but at the same time he was panicking that more would be expected of him than he would be able to deliver.

He was plagued by ambivalence again: sensing that change might, after all, be rewarding, but at the same time fearing the prospect very greatly. His progress was gradual and erratic. But all the time he seemed to go further forward and to regress less.

Held between two people, and without crutches or frame, he had walking practice every morning. He went to the gym for exercises designed to stimulate his leg muscles. He bicycled on a stationary bicycle, managing tiny distances but a little further week by week.

He would always be pressed to participate in social skills training sessions. If assertiveness were being practised, and a pair of shoes being returned to a shop, David would have to persuade some belligerent manager that his shoes were faulty. If someone were being shown ways of dealing with bullying, David would be asked to act the part of the bully—even though after one attempt someone else would be tactfully substituted. If we were working on holding your own in an argument—stating an opinion whatever the opposition—David would be forced out of his habit of assent, and told that everything he said must be prefaced by, 'I disagree.'

I can remember once saying that I didn't want to do it, and all they did was just push the chair out, and it was—umm—terrifying. But I think I just came to realize there was no way I could get out of it so I would have to do something. So the initial fear did wane a bit. And you just had to do it.

You definitely did feel under attack.

But the significant experience for me was to see that 'attack' prompted action, and did not make David crumble, as part of me feared. Teachers all too often fear that if they press the retiring to come forth in public, they will prompt collapse, demoralization, even breakdown.

I asked David how the initial feeling of being under attack began to moderate.

My initial thing was that they were getting at me, and then I began to feel it was getting to know what I could do, seeing for myself what was possible in certain situations. It wasn't comfortable; I don't think it was meant to be.

Looking back, I suppose it was a gradual build-up of confidence. Seeing staff as enemies receded towards the end. But my initial reaction was to try to avoid taking part.

Of course there was a lot of attention on you anyway in the whole place. You had to get used to it, there was no way you couldn't.

I asked, 'Was there a stage when some of the things you did well began to feel good?'

I never felt I was glad I'd done it. There was a feeling that—you know, when someone said, oh that was good, or something—I didn't want to reject it immediately, and think what can I do next time to avoid the attention.

No matter whether you were doing things averagely you would still have had some sort of comment made.

In other words, there was no longer any profit in pretending incapacity, which was what he'd done at school, keeping his work mediocre as a guarantee against teachers' interest.

Then after a while—if something was said—I didn't mind doing it [in other words, taking a prominent part in a session: acting in front of other people, showing himself] so much. I don't think I *wanted* to do it any of the time, but, well, I would. I don't think enjoyment's quite the right word. But it was—getting used to it. I didn't want to avoid the sessions quite so much.

I asked, 'Were any of the good comments—the praise—beginning to be at all pleasurable?' David said:

to a certain extent. Though I still got very uneasy.

But for David to say that praise was 'to a certain extent' pleasurable marked an extraordinary advance for someone who had feared the threat of praise in his school classes.

It is important to note, too, that David took part in these sessions, filmed on video, in front of a group of people that could sometimes be as large as twenty. There would always be plenty of staff taking part, and often visitors as well.

All the time, he was, as he suggests, learning what he could do: learning that people did not engulf him when he disagreed with them: that it was possible to talk to someone and look them in the eye without being rejected; that it was even possible to shout at someone, discover that they would shout back, and that even if they did, he would survive. Gradually he was learning that making contact with other people could be, if not a positive pleasure, then at least not terrifying.

We were learning, too. The person David showed he could be during some of these sessions was increasingly impressive: firm, decisive, intelligent. It strikes me now as interesting that in school we took quite a long time to realize that David must be more able than his teachers had thought. Certainly we paid him more attention, spent more time with him. But what I found to acknowledge as 'good' was still, I thought, good for someone who was going to pass a few CSEs. *Preconception of his ability still trapped me.*

There was a psychology student working at the Ashby at the time. He and David became friendly. He went with David to his spells in the gym; took over the job of measuring his times, giving him walking practice. He began taking David for real walks in the grounds—slow strolls at David's crutch-pace. On one of these walks he persuaded David to throw away his crutches and walk unaided. He was cagey about how he had achieved this. 'I just asked him to give it a try and he did,' was about his reticent limit.

David could not walk far, and his legs were very stiff; but he never used sticks or crutches again.

Shortly afterwards, we had a social skills session designed to be more fun than most. We decided to enact a court scene. We elected a criminal, who had broken into a shop in broad daylight; chose several eye-witnesses, counsel for the defence, a prosecutor, a judge, and as many of a jury as we could muster. David was prosecutor. Asked to volunteer for a part, he wouldn't, so we chose for him. We were pleased to see him put up more opposition to this pressure than usual: it was good to provoke ordinary anger instead of dumb acceptance. But Stephen was adamant, as usual. He told David there was no one who could do the job better. David had no choice but to accept.

Angered, he was brilliant. The tape has long since been erased, and I cannot recall the details of his grilling of witnesses and his contemptuous dismissal of the plaintiff's attempts to get off the hook, and of the defending lawyer's attempts to hoodwink; but I do recall that he was applauded when the criminal went down for a heavy sentence. David was fluent, articulate, aggressive; and used a vocabulary we never suspected he possessed.

The penny dropped. I have to admit the irony—which I think speaks volumes about my still unshed conditioning as a comprehensive teacher—of being finally convinced of his high intelligence, not by hints in his written work, or by his quick understanding of people's moods and feelings or by his dry wit, but by hearing him use elaborate words so fluently. Mine was a thoroughly pedagogic revelation. 'Manifestly absurd', he said of some statement that had failed to convince him. I wish I had written down some of the words he used. But I imagine, now, startling embellishments of his case—words like 'perfidious' or 'mendacity'.

We talked and talked about what we could do in school to encourage David to express his ability in his academic work. In the end we decided to put him in for three O levels, as well as the CSEs he was due to take soon. The syllabus for history O level was not greatly different from the syllabus he had been studying for CSE, so history was one choice. English language was another—because I suddenly wanted a chance to prove to him that he could perform on paper as fluently as he had done in court.

We were lucky at that time to have an afternoon a week of teaching by Katherine, an artist. I've known few so gifted at luring talent and skill from the demoralized and the reluctant. She found that David was a competent draughtsman; so we decided that art should be the third O level.

For the first time in my life I was excited by an exam. I taught him intensively for the next six weeks. To begin with he was incredulous, sure he would never reach the required standard, when we told him our plans. But we assured him he had nothing to lose, since he would be taking the CSEs as well.

His English improved hectically. I do not need complicated statistical studies to prove 'the expectancy effect'—the effect that a heightened expectation can have on a pupil's performance. Teaching David offered me proof enough.

We began with simple things. Some of his regular spelling mistakes began to disappear. He probably thought that he would muddle 'to', 'too' and 'two' for the rest of his life; but we devised a checking system that put him in command of that fault as well as many others. He used, for instance, to miss the 'e' out of words ending in 'ed'. No longer. It astonished and delighted me that such rudimentary conquests could give him so much confidence. He began, encouraged, to write essays about his own experience, rather than the dead, stock pieces he had produced before.

In history, knowledge and interest emerged and overwhelmed his timidity and his reluctance to express opinions; and I soon realized that O level was easily within his reach.

He began to talk more, still quietly, but so that teaching him became far more rewarding.

He managed a B for history, a C for art, and just failed his English with a D.

His metamorphosis was assured—from someone defined as not particularly intelligent, and unlikely to do well academically, to a different sort of person altogether, whose success continued.

After leaving us, he went not back to school, but to a college of further education, where classes were smaller and he found himself treated with the same energy, interest, and attention as we, in the end, had offered him. There he took and passed more O levels, including English. Most startling of all his early achievements there was to pass maths O level at his second attempt, after being treated at school as almost innumerate.

Shortly after I first interviewed him, his A level results came out. He achieved a B for English, a B for sociology and a C for history.

Why David changed, and the train of thought he started

Since for David it was contact with other people, and being noticed, that were such frightening experiences, his successful evasion in school served his immediate interests very well. Had we not forced ourselves upon him; had we not kept our nerve when he did his best to make us feel cruel; had we not demanded that he learn that contact with other people would not kill him, as his phantasies may have suggested; had we not flushed his intellect out of cover and told him to put it to use—had we not *acknowledged* him in his uniqueness, *his long-term interests would have been ill-served indeed.*

He was lucky to break down. I have worked with many adolescents in distress of whom that can later be aptly said. It was his breakdown that forced him to be noticed; though even when in range of our therapeutic vigilance, there was a long phase during which he began to be seen as irretrievably withdrawn, and to be taken for granted as intellectually what his school claimed. Had it not been for the paralysis itself, which eventually fuelled our impatience, our irritability, our anger, our refusal to be defeated—had it not been for that hysterical demand to be noticed—David might never have developed. For what someone needs who is so carefully protected by masks and feints and deceits, is, above all, to be noticed.

David took on the theory that he was so inadequate, uninteresting, vulnerable and useless that he might as well lose the use of his legs, for what was the point of their lugging such a creature around. Perhaps because he was really a strong and intelligent person, he opted for an experiment, in the end, which was bound to disprove his theory. Disprove it, it did; his hysterical paralysis led him through rejection of his theory of inadequacy (or at any rate made it very difficult for him to continue to believe it) towards a new theory; of high intelligence, social competence, and the strength to withstand some severe psychological demands.

Not all who need one achieve a new theory. It was the predicament of those not as lucky as David which began to interest me.

My friend and colleague Mary and I became almost obsessed by the implications of David's school career. The experience of teaching him was very startling. Neither of us had known such a complete reversal of expectation before.

David prompted in us reminiscence about our own teaching experience in ordinary secondary schools. We felt retrospective guilt: we knew that his breakthrough could never have taken place in a comprehensive or a grammar school. We knew that in our old lives as pedagogic drudges, we would have continued to assume—had he been a member of one of our classes—that he was what he presented himself to be: a shy neurotic kind of boy without much ability. We knew, above all, that we would never have had a chance of realizing what enormous intelligence had gone into that camouflage, that evasion, that subtle and persistent discretion.

No. For us he would have been a dud.

We had in common nostalgia for the days when we used to tread the boards of our classrooms, taming the back rows and seducing the front, garlanded by good exam results and sweetened by the smiles of our favourites. Considering the sort of teachers we were, David, we knew, would not have had a look in: what could he have given us, immune as he would have been to our enthusiasm, our jokes, the tatty old third-rate-music-hall routines of the shameless pedagogue?

We talked a great deal about this common experience of being histrionic teachers. We could acknowledge that we'd both been good at it; but David's case made us wonder what exactly we had been good at. We swapped stories of our successes and our popularity, like Russian exiles talking about their lost estates. We acknowledged that there was nothing more satisfying as a teacher than to like and be liked; and nothing more dreary than to be faced with the torpid, biddable faces of the unresponsive.

At about this time we held a seminar for our colleagues about 'classroom geography'. We had been asked to gather our thoughts about what some of our patients might have been like in their ordinary schools: what sort of lives they might have led in school, and how teachers might have seen them.

We began to think about ordinary classrooms, and the question we asked ourselves was this: if classes are conventional—lines of pupils facing teachers—then where, given a certain amount of choice, will different sorts of pupils sit? We decided that the subversive sit at the back, and the actively co-operative near the front. So far so obvious— or so it seemed to us. But the thought which intrigued us most was that the shy and retiring and frightened, those then in the majority at the Ashby—those like David—would, if possible, sit at the sides of the room.

It interests me now, after writing my account of my early teaching experience, with its revelations of partiality towards some and anonymity for many, that we took for granted *as a premiss* that teachers *do* allocate their attention unequally, and that many will seek to avoid it.

It seemed to us likely that teachers would have most to do with those who sit before them in an arrangement like a bottle—with a wide bottom to take in the back row. The neck of the bottle would be the middle portions of the front three or four rows, where would sit the most eager and co-operative. There would be blind spots outside the bottle's neck, where the evasive would be particularly safe; and seats near the sides of the room would also be outside the bottle.

It is important to recall this discussion that preceded our seminar; because after the discovery of the teaching bottle, I could not think about ordinary classrooms or about my teaching experience in the same way ever again.

I had thought myself independent, undetermined; that I had made choices about what had gone on in my classes which had been demonstrations of my freedom. But David had manipulated his teachers—just as someone sitting to the side of a room manipulates his teachers not to see him. None of David's teachers had been free to see him as he really was or could be—without a revision of perception, a readjustment of attention that they had obviously not been able to make.

Dimly I began to sense that the game I had been playing so blindly had been constrained, restricted, ritualized. I sensed that there had been many limits put upon my freedom. A crucial stage had been reached in my own growing awareness of what I'd been doing for so long: I began to think of classes not as the recipients of my learning, the raw material on which I exercised my skill, but as possessing a life of their own, the complexity of which I had not begun to understand when I worked in comprehensives.

The great fallacy

I had, too, begun to free myself from a fallacy: teachers, from the beginning of their training, are persuaded that they really *can* teach all their pupils with equal success. Parents expect teachers to do so, and to know all children in their uniqueness. This is impossible. But a philosophy underpins the expectation: that pupils come to school in order that they shall flourish as individuals. Their talents will be discovered and cultivated; measure will be taken of their intellects which will be appropriately stimulated to ensure the fullest possible development. Schools are engines for the fulfilment of individuals.

The fallacy is that, burdened with this expectation, imbued with the liberal philosophy that underpins it, teachers facing classes believe that they are facing individuals. They are not; they are facing crowds, and individuals in crowds are not all equally accessible, equally visible.

Despite what they may learn about the constitution and behaviour of crowds, the expectation that they will teach and know individuals with equal thoroughness, and the belief that that is what they should be doing, are too strong: teachers tend to treat their classes as collections of individuals, about whom they feel empowered to make confident claims and predictions. When their pupils behave in certain ways, they will all too often attribute their behaviour to deficiencies or splendours in those pupils' personalities; just as they tend to attribute their pupils' academic performances to the possession or absence of quantifiable, static abilities.

In other words, they talk about their pupils, their behaviour, and their academic performances *as if* they are talking of each one as someone known and understood in an ordinary relationship between two people, meeting and experiencing each other 'one to one'. They do indeed relate to some pupils in this way; but not to all. The trouble is that teachers tend to talk about all pupils, known well—acknowledged—and known hardly at all, with the same confidence, the same certainty that they can be described and explained.

This betokens a split in teachers' thinking: a gulf between what their experience tells them, and what they say about that experience. They know perfectly well that they cannot allocate time and attention equally, and that they cannot know all their pupils thoroughly—look how easily Mary and I established the premiss of unequal distribution of attention. Daily, experience proves these impossibilities. And yet they describe, explain, interpret all individuals as if these impossibilities did not exist.

It is as if teachers, guilty about their limitations—not their own fault, but the result of their circumstances—deny that guilt, and pretend there are no limitations.

The experience of being in a crowd—and being in a large school— influenced Alasdair to complicated concealment of his individuality. But I sought him out as one individual seeking out another; and when baffled, I turned not to examination of my own limiting circumstances, nor to social psychology, but to adjectives with which I could then dismiss him: limited, shy, lazy. And I used them confidently, as if they were adequate description of someone I had fathomed. My ignorance of him—secured by his evasions—should have prevented me from attempting *any* convinced definition of *any* aspect of his personality or intelligence.

A teacher does not face individuals, but *versions* of individuals, each version tailored to suit the individual's particular needs in the particular predicament of being in school. The attractive and open and readily acknowledged are probably showing versions of themselves that are close to their true potential; the concealed and evasive versions very far from their possible selves.

Each version is designed to test a particular hypothesis expressive in varying degrees of the worth and potential of the person concerned.

This is what I began, dimly, to realize. It is interesting that while I was still immersed in the experience of being in a school, I could not realize it; I needed to be taken out of schools and put into completely different circumstances in order to do so; to be dislocated in order to understand where I had been.

An analogy is needed. I could not hope to work effectively on a submarine. I am by nature slightly paranoiac. Anxiety can sometimes overwhelm me. I am also claustrophobic, a very poor sailor, and some- one for whom some privacy and solitude are essential.

My behaviour and performance as a submariner would be determined by my unsuitability. I might cope; but I would not impress; and most of my energy would go into coping, so that I would have little over for competence. I would be daunted, subdued, and perhaps forced provi- sionally into a depressingly meagre hypothesis of my own worth. But being adult, I might just be able to distance myself enough to say: it's the submarine, not me; on land I could be another person.

Submariners are carefully selected; but everyone goes to school. And *schools are as unlike the rest of life as is a submarine.*

CHAPTER THREE

Anne and Paul abandoned in Nomansland

Nomansland

Two years after teaching David, I was accepted by a university department to research the predicament in secondary schools of the biddable, compliant and unremarkable. That was my starting point.

To begin with, I interviewed David. By that time I was preoccupied by an idea of the middle ground of large classes: I had decided that it was useful to think of a 'nomansland' in a large class, where pupils could conceal themselves for a variety of reasons. 'Nomansland' I conceived as a social and psychological refuge—not necessarily to be found at the edges of large classes, though to sit outside the 'bottle' would be to make the refuge safer.

Nomansland offers protection from attention and activity, which an escaping pupil seeks and preserves by means of the sort of tactics used by David: assiduously maintained mediocrity in work of just sufficient quantity to escape rebuke; lowered gaze; making your presence as unrewarding as possible when contact with a teacher is finally unavoidable.

To find out more about Nomansland, about why people end up there and what happens when they do, I looked for more people to talk to about their school careers. I wanted to find people who had not been particularly successful or remarkable; who were neither particularly satisfied nor particularly praised. Most of all I hoped to find ex-pupils who had themselves sought refuge in Nomansland.

I found several at David's FE college. I was lucky. His sociology teacher was interested in my work, and invited me to come to the college, and, first of all, to talk to her A level students. From that class I recruited about half who were willing and keen to talk about their school careers; and subsequently several of the others volunteered. They were eager to have an opportunity to talk about experience that was still fresh—for most—but about which they now felt they had some sort of objectivity. Like exiles who feel that they now understand their homeland for the first time, they seemed to feel that now that they had left school, they could at last see through and interpret the dominant experience of their lives so far. And I caught them at a time when that process of interpretation was crucially important; was for many of them part of the stage of growing up which they had by then reached.

The majority had left school a year ago, before taking A levels. The majority had come from comprehensive schools without sixth forms; and their choice at the end of their fifth year had been to go to college, or to the sixth form of a local grammar school, not yet itself turned into a comprehensive. Most chose college because of a vague sense of being fed up with school, of wanting a more adult atmosphere. Some were far from vague about this choice:

I couldn't stand school. I wanted to get some more O levels to join the RAF. I couldn't stand any more of the school atmosphere, I wanted to be treated more as an individual, more as an adult . . .

I soon realized how lucky I was. I was interested in finding out about what school had been like for those who had not shone academically, nor had been difficult and demanding. I wanted to know more about the sort of pupils I had so thoroughly forgotten; those whose books I had marked but whose souls had remained obscure to me. In the area which served the college, those who had already shone at their work tended to go to the grammar school; those who had been deviant and difficult did not at that stage want more education. I had stumbled on a group of people— for in the end I talked to some from other classes, taking either O or A levels—who with two exceptions had belonged to just the group in which I was interested.

I must make clear what made them a coherent group. What they had in common was lack of clear achievement. None had achieved quite what they had hoped they would achieve, or their teachers had earlier said they would achieve, or their parents had hoped they would achieve. They were unfulfilled; not yet clear about the extent of their own abilities.

I discovered that their teachers at the FE college made a speciality of just that sort of exhortation that pupils need when their confidence ebbs. They were used to students who had a lack of belief in themselves, and no clear idea of what they might achieve; skilled at persuading people that they had nothing to lose by assuming—just for the moment—that they *were* capable of success; that it *was* worth their while to think more highly of themselves. They were strategists and tacticians of the presentation of fresh theories of themselves to people whose old ones badly needed replacement.

Anne was in her mid-thirties, and one of the most interesting people I have talked to about their school careers.

I came here actually to do O level, but they persuaded me to do A level and my husband encouraged me.

I asked her if at first she hadn't liked the idea.

I didn't think I was clever enough to tackle anything like that. It started off [her return to education] taking two O levels in the evening, and I sort of intended to do the same here—I thought, oh, I'll take a couple more O levels since I know I can do them—I didn't want to do A levels.

But her husband persuaded her. She took sociology and English, having failed English O level at school.

With all the jargon and everything in the sociology classes, I was thinking of pulling out in the first two weeks, but it was a friendly atmosphere, and I talked to M—[the teacher], and she said try it for a bit longer, and now I really enjoy it.

The students' school careers tended also to be changeable. Common to most of their accounts is nostalgia for a time when things had gone particularly well, usually early on in school. A subject had interested them, and been taught by a teacher who had liked them, for instance; or one year in particular had been full of success. Nostalgia might be for a school, a subject, a teacher, or a subject as it had once been taught.

Similarly, they had experienced a great deal of disappointment, most of it at secondary school, none of it on the whole glaring, but vague, insidious, elusive. Many of them, too, had been victims of boredom; and most had at one stage opted out of participation, competition, activity.

Their accounts reflect the volatility of adolescence as a time of life. They exemplify the idea that in adolescence we try out theories about ourselves; but, startlingly, they exemplify too that schools and teachers are not well equipped to cope with change in their pupils; particularly from willingness and interest to passivity and disenchantment.

Many of those I talked to 'slid' into passivity when—usually—just fifteen. At that point, rescue would have needed acknowledgement. Instead, when they slid, they met from teachers disappointment, disengagement, lack of interest.

What I wanted from those I interviewed, and what they so richly provided, were their stories. So many of the children I had taught had had stories to tell about their school careers of which I had no inkling; and about those same pupils I had made confident but inaccurate assumptions.

I cannot emphasize too strongly the confidence with which teachers judge their pupils. Even their tentativeness can be confident. When they say, 'I don't know what makes this girl tick,' they are often really saying, 'This is the sort of girl who tick is mysterious, *you* know.' One reason for this confidence, this certainty, is that teachers are *expected* to know their pupils, and will fabricate certainty rather than admit ignorance.

The hunt for credentials is also to blame. If you are teaching pupils to pass a public examination, you are for ever obliged to judge their work according to a required standard. Because adolescence can be a difficult time, and because adolescents are so changeable, a hard-pressed teacher with a large syllabus to get through can never judge a piece of work without at the same time exhorting or warning or deploring or praising, aware that pupils may so suddenly falter or fade.

'This is really not good enough . . .'

' "A lot" is nursery talk, and you should have grown out of it.'

'. . . excellent piece of work; however I think you should have paid more attention to . . .'

These statements are from a teacher's awareness that her pupils need to be kept at it. And it is more difficult to make the right sort of statement—the right mix of exhortation, caution, praise and horror—if your mind is open. But if you decide that you *know* your pupil, you will be able to say what she needs to hear, or is capable of hearing.

The need to assess in order to get on with the job of getting credentials, can force presumption. So can the need to *control* crowds of twenty-five or more pupils. An effective teacher has to be a good crowd-controller. This is often difficult, to say the least. She has to be diplomat, sergeant-major, mother, father, entertainer. One of her strongest weapons is clear knowledge of her pupils. The strict teachers who lurk in many people's memories were for ever saying, 'I know your little game . . . don't think I don't know what you're up to, I know you through and through . . .' They were for ever smiling thin omniscient smiles as they read your work, so that you feared they could read your mind; for ever anticipating, being one step ahead, claiming authoritatively that they knew everything about you.

Teachers become know-alls because of years of knowing more about their subjects than do those they teach, but also because of being forced to pretend certain knowledge of their pupils' characters and capacities. Knowledge of subject and knowledge of pupils are power; and to win the class war, teachers need power.

I want now to give a very brief account of an early experience at the Ashby Unit which showed me how thoroughly I had been trained as a teacher to jump to conclusions.

Sandy

Sandy came to us because his school claimed they could no longer control him. He had had a year off school a year before, after a serious car accident.

Before he arrived, I imagined a familiar adolescent disaster: a boy grown too quickly to strength he did not yet understand, confused by sex, backward, alarmed by the chaos he seemed to produce around him without knowing how or why. With the familiarity of this story came familiar doubts. I suspected that I would be able to do very little for him as a teacher. It was as if I'd decided that I knew him before we had even met.

He turned out to be smaller than I had expected: a short, strong, tubby figure with red hair. He assaulted everyone with dirty jokes.

'What goes in dry and comes out wet?' he would shout to me, running up to me in a corridor, grabbing my arm, and peering at me far too closely for comfort.

'Come on, Sandy,' I'd say, 'I really don't want to know just now.'

'A teabag,' he'd say. 'You've got a filthy mind!'

He was very young for his age, sometimes infantile. Given work to do that he didn't like, his sulk was an omnipotent infant's. But we would ignore him. Neglected, he would rampage, interrupt, tease; but would do as asked in the end, with a bad grace. I found it easy to imagine the havoc he might create in an ordinary classroom where such canny tactics were usually far more difficult to put into practice.

He'd had far too much attention, we decided: too much at home—which was not surprising, since his accident had nearly killed him; and too much at school, once he had become an intractable problem. When expected to be difficult, pupils often are.

A meeting was arranged with his headmistress. Stephen, the psychologist, a doctor, and I were to go to Sandy's school for this. We told her that we would try to modify Sandy's behaviour, and she reluctantly agreed that she would have him back in school for a trial period when we said he was ready.

In the car again afterwards, Stephen began to talk about what we could do for Sandy. We agreed that he had no idea of the sanctity of 'personal space'—he invaded everyone's, grabbing arms, hands, shoulders inappropriately. Sometimes he'd kissed nurses at the Ashby, when talking to them, like a very young child. It was as if, socially, physically, he behaved like a 4-year-old. Stephen said we should put him on a programme, for which we would decide what behaviour to ignore or rebuff, and what to acknowledge warmly or praise.

I couldn't contain my scepticism. Sandy had only two years' schooling to go. He would be fixed in a role, a way of behaving in school. I *knew* what he would be like in a classroom—and was sure that the habits he'd acquired would be too fixed to change. I knew what such boys were like; I'd taught dozens like him, and tried to change them, and it was never any good. I said all this, and Stephen was angry.

'Christ, you bloody teachers, you're all the same, pessimistic bloody know-alls—I'm fed up with it—we get something going, get excited by it, and you tell us it's doomed to fail—it really pisses me off.'

New to the staff, I felt severely put down. Stephen was an established and powerful member of staff whom I liked and respected. Determined to show I was not a gloomy, pessimistic, stick-in-the-mud teacher, I took a very active part in Sandy's programme, and was in the end forgiven.

Sandy grew up. That is what his change amounted to. He stopped racing up to people with dirty jokes, forcing his face so close to yours as he spoke that you had to back away.

One social skills session was crucial. I shall describe it, since it exemplifies the efficacy of social skills training.

With perhaps fifteen staff and patients as actors, we mocked up a classroom scene, and told Sandy to do everything he could to make a nuisance of himself. Patients and staff were pupils, and one member of staff played the part of the teacher. Sandy threw things, spat, inter-rupted, did the opposite of what he was asked, farted, belched, attacked other pupils. All this was filmed on videotape.

Then we replayed the tape and asked Sandy what he thought of his behaviour. He talked like an adult about it, and said that he had been bloody awful and he didn't think anyone should have to put up with him. We persuaded him to talk about the past month in the Ashby, and told him he was beginning to be better company. A boy said Sandy was beginning to be 'normal' and not shout all the time.

We asked him why his school had wanted to chuck him out. He didn't want to talk about this, but eventually admitted that it was because he had 'acted up' all the time. What was the worst thing he'd done, we asked. Trying for bravado, laughing uneasily, he told us that 'they'—his friends—had dared him to flash at a teacher. He hadn't really, he'd only unzipped his fly.

Nobody laughed. He looked very uncomfortable. We said nothing, but played the tape of the discussion. We asked Sandy to consider the difference between his behaviour in the classroom and the way he talked to us afterwards. Everyone voted on which Sandy they preferred. All chose the second. The first was variously described as 'a pain in the arse', 'a kid', 'boring', and 'bloody awful'.

Similar, potent unanimity met all his behaviour. When he had conversations with us free of dirty jokes and intrusive pawing, we would tell him how much we had enjoyed talking to him. He was helpful and kind with one very distressed psychotic girl, and we could thank him for that. Rebuff or inattention when he lapsed were equally unanimous; not cold or rejecting, but implacable none the less.

He began to be his age; and instead of feeling that I was a behaviourist manipulator—I'd been prejudiced against behaviour modification before working at the Ashby—I felt I was helping to apply common sense; accelerating and condensing a social education that should have taken place in Sandy's ordinary life, but hadn't.

I learned that my assumptions, and particularly my assumptions about his probable chances back in school, had been wrong. They were based on a too ready interpretation of too little evidence. He seemed 'that type' of boy, so I assumed that he would behave accordingly, whatever was done to try to help him not to do so—and it was useless to pretend otherwise.

I'd been far too quick to be certain about him. He went back to school after two months with us. He survived his last two years. The speed and glibness of my assumptions had been typically those of a teacher. Stephen had been right: I'd been behaving like a know-all.

So, when I listened to the students at David's college telling me about their schooling, I remembered that teachers are forced to judge, and to judge quickly and often wrongly. I wanted to keep teachers in mind as I listened: I wanted to understand how teachers confirm evasion, anonymity, and disappearance in Nomansland.

Anne and Paul

These two make an interesting pair. Anne I met and interviewed because she was in David's classes, and a friend of his. Paul was in the year below them, but was being taught by David's sociology teacher.

It would be hard to design two people more different in character than Anne and Paul. Anne was in her mid-thirties, and a mother; Paul was 23 and unmarried. Anne I instantly liked when I first met her. She impressed me, too, because she found it difficult to talk freely, and yet she offered to try. As her story developed I became more and more impressed—by the fortitude that had led her back into education. She was tall, slight, with long blond hair often curtaining her face, her manner a mixture of shyness and forcefulness, as if she were constantly willing herself to break through her reluctance to speak and be noticed.

Paul was in every way different. He was stout, forthright, amused, untroubled, optimistic. He talked fluently and with little prompting. I felt that Anne talked against her desire to be silent. Her manner, her story, and her success spoke determination to change herself and her life that was very moving. Paul also wanted to change his life, but everything about him suggested that his determination had been easier to come by.

Both of them were now taking A levels: Anne—English and sociology; Paul—English, history and sociology. Neither had achieved more than two O levels at school.

Anne came back into education fifteen years after leaving school, first to evening classes where she took and passed two more O levels, then full-time to FE college, where at first, as I have already said, she did not think herself capable of taking A levels. Paul left school and went straight to the same FE college, to sit and pass three more O levels— which he needed to be accepted as an employee by an insurance firm, where he worked for the next five years. After that:

I was in a rut. I wasn't going to get any further there, however long I stayed. I was ambitious, I wanted change, I wanted something different and that was the best way.

Anne's reasons for coming back into education were less clear. They were partly, she says, to do with lack of confidence in her life. She felt that if:

I actually learnt something I could cope with life better.

At school, both were in what I have characterized as Nomansland: that part of large classes where pupils find accurate self-estimate most difficult to achieve.

Anne's schooling

Anne's story of her schooling is horrifying. She says that she has always been 'perhaps a particularly cautious person'; and she implies that from the start she was, perhaps, excessively fearful at school. But I would find it hard to interpret her fear or timidity as wholly to do with her. Her junior school sounds as if it did a great deal to teach her terror.

The boys always made rude remarks about me, about my clothes and appearance. And there was one boy who used to wait for me outside school and he used to give me a good kicking.

She says that she learnt early to keep her head down and not ask questions. From early in her schooling, concealment was her aim, from which she never wavered.

I suspect she was someone to whom bullies were naturally attracted: someone troubled, apart, afraid.

There was a particular group of boys who would sort of home in.

Of all the horrors school can provide, the persecution comfortingly known as bullying must be the worst. What a euphemism the word is, implying something English, robust, admirable—suggestive of experience all must endure if their characters are to fledge. I was never much bullied at school, but my imagination is strong enough to flinch from the thought of Anne going to school every day to be at the mercy of a group of boys who 'homed in' on her.

From a bus recently, I saw a small boy being bullied by four much bigger boys. I had noticed him before on other bus journeys: he was odd-looking, with a domed forehead, very small eyes, and the hunched shoulders of a little old man. His baiters were slugging him—not very hard—with their school bags, walking round him lazily to do so; and he was slugging them back with his bag. His lunges looked pathetic, despairing, ineffectual; but his baiters never missed. And they went on and on and on, during the two minutes I watched, my bus jammed in traffic. They were so much bigger than he was; and the expression on their faces was lazy and sensual, their craving to hurt being visibly appeased.

Children are stoical. He would be back in school the next day for more, or the threat of more. And Anne, just the same, went back and back.

She took and failed the eleven-plus, and went first to an all-girls' school, a comprehensive. Here she had the one brief pleasurable interlude in her school career. She benefited from her anonymity and from the lack of boys. Her golden age was brief and ironic: it was as if she could use the discretion she had learnt in her first school to get on with her work in peace. There were no boys to bully her; and she was by chance in what she describes as a 'well-organized school'.

I suspect that this phrase, at a great distance in time, reflects her lasting perception of this first secondary school as a place where she could enjoy peace. 'Well-organized' suggests that her days were for the first time without the unpredictable; were safe from malevolence, persecution, and incursions of sudden chaotic dangers. It was a time of convalescence, which she enjoyed. Had it continued, the intellectual revolution which had to wait till her mid-thirties, might have taken off.

Intellectual growth cannot take place without self-esteem, sufficient contentment to free the mind to work, a strong relationship with an adult who acknowledges you, and peace in the place where you learn. It is that peace that Anne possessed for the first time in her school career.

She remembers:

They had a kind of form magazine, and I don't know how I did it, but I ended up taking the thing over. At the end it was my cover, my editing, and full of mostly my writing.

It was a completely different environment from my primary school, and because nobody knew me I didn't mind trying.

By this she means there were no hostile and familiar boys who would laugh at her efforts and bully her for them. I asked:

'Did you feel good as a result?'

'Oh yes, I felt really good.'

'And then you moved?'

'Yes.'

She moved; and in her new—mixed—school, she had once again to use her anonymity and her considerable skill at self-camouflage to sur-vive, rather than to work. Her mind was no longer free and contented, but monopolized by anxiety, and by the need to hide—in Nomansland.

She used David's tactics to survive in a tough, embattled school in Inner London where, her memory tells her, the 'only way teachers knew of controlling people was shouting all the time'.

This is the key memory of the second secondary school to set against the memory of the first as 'well-organized'. In the first she could relax and extend herself because the school had organized peace for her. But of the second she remembers *shouting teachers*—a vivid memory of the opposite of organized peace. For adults to have to shout is a sign of the power, the danger, and the unpredictability of what they have to con-trol; is a sign of the absence of organized peace. In its place was a struggle to contain war. She had exchanged a library for a battlefield.

She made friends with a few girls. But she could not afford to relax her vigilance. One friend sat next to her in her English class. Not daring to answer herself, she:

used to feed answers to my friend. I was very careful in class. I would sit out of the way, keep quiet. It's quite easy to avoid answering questions: you look down or out of the window; and I grew my hair long—couldn't see through it. For years I had long hair; I only recently cut it.

To my enormous interest and satisfaction, she said she always chose, if she could, to sit at the side, near the front.

So, she fed answers to her friend.

But the trouble was that it wasn't the sort of school where it was okay to be academically bright, so a group of girls got together and beat her up on the way home from school—because she'd been getting good feedback from the teacher for answering well.

This incident put a stop even to this indirect participation.

I wanted to answer so much. I wasn't going to do it myself. But after that I stopped altogether.

I have talked of pupils whose energy and intelligence seem to be used solely for evasion, for survival. It seems to me easy to understand why Anne had no energy left for anything else. Her teachers were no help. None acknowledged her; none noticed her promise. She failed English O level—and years later got a B for A level.

School became a 'chore' to be 'got through'; and she was 'very very bored'. When it came to choose which subjects to specialize in, she didn't know which to pick. She wanted to do biology, but this would have meant taking chemistry and physics as well, and so she took languages instead. Her parents had been told at a parents' evening that girls didn't need maths, so she didn't take that subject either. In the end, she was entered for three O levels, and passed two.

Her failure at English may be attributed to her imprisonment in anxiety, but also to the teacher she was unfortunate enough to have.

He was very domineering. He said you can't write stories any more, you're not juniors any more, you've got to base your essays on fact. He had this horrible technique, you'd write an essay and he'd pick it out, and you knew it had been awful anyway, and he'd read it out to the class in the most sarcastic and denigrating way possible. You'd practically crawl out of the classroom in the end. I became so terrified of writing essays I couldn't express myself at all. And when I took the O level, I can remember looking at the list of essays in blind panic, thinking I can't do any of them.

I suspect that, when they noticed her at all, her teachers saw what they took to be a timid girl of no great interest.

She managed to avoid attention, and to be left to herself; to accept a hypothesis of her worth and ability much lower than the ideas of herself that her husband and her teachers at FE college eventually managed to persuade her to accept—ideas that must be even harder to reject now she has gained entrance to a university.

I said to her rather lamely, 'It must have been a bad school.'

Well, I would agree with you there. In fact, later on when my daughter was choosing her school, I said to my husband that if she had to go to a school like that, I wouldn't let her go—and he couldn't understand. He said you could go to prison for a thing like that, and I said, well I would, because I feel so strongly about it. Mainly because I would want her to enjoy education rather than be frightened by it, it's so unpleasant that it could destroy a person. I feel, you know, that school life actually destroyed my personality—and I get very upset when I talk about it.

Anne's failure was quiet and undemonstrative. She turned away from her one chance of high expectations, the interest of teachers, and academic ambition—to a discontented, passive, fearful mediocrity.

Her story, taken with David's, is illustration of a common predicament in Nomansland: some seek its protective anonymity because school makes them afraid and anxious. Their fear and anxiety may be extreme, even pathological—as one could argue David's was; or can be more explicable, as in Anne's case, the result of bullying and inability to withstand the pressures of a tough school. But whatever the origin of anxiety, it is school that allows it to breed; and the effects are the same: stifled talent, an unheard voice, and an unacknowledged individual.

Paul

One of the most interesting features of Nomansland is the variety of its population. Paul's reasons for being there were very different from Anne's.

The only time Anne ever spoke up for herself was when her time came in the fifth year to be a prefect. She refused. The idea of such prominence was so abhorrent to her, she broke through her silence and timidity, and refused. But when Paul was not made a perfect at the same stage in his school career, he was upset and disappointed.

He was, he said, neither successful nor unsuccessful at primary school. When he failed the eleven-plus, his father sent him to a local public school. There, a sort of misery began; nothing by his description as grave as Anne's, but misery none the less:

One long horror story from beginning to end.

He says of himself at that time that he was:

An average sort of person, fairly average sort of achievements, and they were way ahead of me.

What he meant was that he found the presence of other bright pupils intimidating. And:

Marks and places were all important—you either had to be good at the work or good at sport. They all became good sportsmen or great brains, and I was neither.

He seems to have decided early on that he was 'thick'.

I was not that good at work and not that good at sport.

I asked, 'What was the evidence?'
    He said:

. . . performances in class. The first term in maths I managed to achieve 5 per cent, and this was a tremendous joke—I didn't find it very amusing.

But although he says of himself at that stage that he was average and that others—such as his best friend who went to Oxford and never had to spend more than a few minutes on his homework—were so much brighter, he also said:

I don't think it was my ability: I didn't fit in well socially. Most of them were from the higher echelons of Catholic society; there were a lot of pupils who boarded, and I was just a local lad—my parents didn't have a title or anything like that.
    In the end I just gave up and didn't try to achieve anything. I just decided in my mind there was no way I was going to do any good.

This caused him distress. His father, not a rich man, was paying his fees, and he wanted to live up to his parents' expectations.
    What interests me most about this first stage of his school career is that he quite clearly treated his early experience as evidence on which to base an interpretation—a theory—of his worth, of himself:

I just decided in my mind there was no way I was going to do any good.

And having made that decision, having accepted that hypothesis, he joined a small group of quiet dissidents for crafty fags, the odd skive off a lesson.
    His theory was: I am not *like them*. He took his difference to be an intellectual one; though he now believes it to have been primarily social. He acknowledges that he has since proved that he has ability. Interestingly, too, nobody made a bid to challenge this faulty theory. He had

been consistently doing well in French; but his success didn't generalize to other subjects; nor did his French teacher use his success to argue a case with his colleagues for Paul being able and intelligent. His success was isolated.

It was my moment of glory when the French master read out that I was doing well [in a weekly mark-reading when he would usually be in the top three]. Then after that, with the rest of them, I could just sit back and know that I was going to come in the bottom two or three of the class.

The reason for this is that teachers do not talk to each other systematically about their pupils—least of all those who do not attract their interest and attention.

It is possible, for instance, to imagine one pupil studying both French and Latin. At Latin she does well—not spectacularly well, but enough to cope with the ruthless complexities of Latin grammar. At French, however, she does poorly. Her Latin teacher gives her moderate praise; her French teacher—in another department—writes in her report, 'I fear that Samantha has no talent for languages.' One brief discussion between the two teachers should lead to the French teacher criticizing her own assumption and trying to find out *why* Samantha was not succeeding; but such a discussion will often not take place, particularly if Samantha is a quiet, nice girl who writes neatly. Paul, though he skived from time to time and smoked, makes it clear that it was just not possible to be glaringly deviant at that first secondary school: he did not become particularly noticeable.

At 13, Paul and his parents agreed that he should leave this school. He went instead to a secondary modern about to become comprehensive. There, to begin with, he was 'punched around' by 'yobbos' who didn't take to his Yorkshire accent—he and his family had moved from North to South. But he learnt to cope with them, and at first, life at this school made his optimism surface.

But by the end of the year, he was disillusioned, disenchanted, bored, passive and idle.

I'd lost interest. It was the school itself, most of the teachers I couldn't get on with, they treated me very much as a child, which by the time I got to my second year there [fourth year of secondary education] I resented a lot.

I was a little kid in their eyes, I was just part of the job, like a test-tube is part of the job—a kid was just there as another instrument of education.

I never had any sort of rapport or relationship with them. Relationships didn't seem to be an important factor, there were very few. The ones who were best at the class-work tended to get on well with the subject teacher.

They joined, in other words, these teachers' 'families'. And his overall remembered impression of teachers:

There was a low level of interest, they didn't really care, they'd got no interest in what was going on, they were there to do their job and earn their money, which was fair enough, I suppose, but they'd got no real extra interest in the kids at all.

Teachers' family members would presumably not have subscribed to such condemnation. 'Just there to do their job and earn their money' is a comment by an unacknowledged pupil on teachers who pay him little attention. What attention they do give him is routine, obligatory, uninterested in him as a person. They 'do their job' with him, but no more. That 'more', that 'extra', what I have called 'subtle partiality', is perhaps the most important of teachers' offerings to their pupils.

I asked Paul how important he thought 'real extra interest in the kids' was:

Oh, it's immensely important. If you think the teacher's not going to bother, you're not going to bother yourself.

He gives us a lucid statement of what it's like not to be acknowledged for what you feel yourself to be: in his case, older than his teachers seemed to think he was.

I think I grew up quicker than they seemed to give me credit for.

He felt himself to be a different person from the one they saw; they did not look closely enough to see what he really was.

And he did nothing, and nor did they, to prise off the theory that he was academically average, ordinary, a bit of a dud. He brought this theory with him from his previous school, and it stayed.

I did what was required of me and not one inch more, and I didn't do any less either. I carried on on the straight and narrow, tried not to upset anybody, but I didn't try to impress anybody.

This is a perfect statement of the prevailing intention of Nomansland: a wish, by using the disguise of moderation and mediocrity, to avert attention. Passivity is safe; doing is dangerous.

I was absolutely passive, I just sat back. I'd never volunteer an answer, I'd never take an active part in discussion.

Like Anne, he gave no trouble—though the path he trod he chose for very different reasons from hers: he was not afraid and anxious. He gave no trouble—so what was the point of disturbing him, of meddling with his torpid brain, of provoking and challenging him to be more active? His teachers, after all, would have had plenty of the wrong sort of activity to cope with.

But he was someone crying out for activity, challenge, responsibility. Near home, he ran a scout troop.

I was the leader, I was in charge of it—and I was still at school! I was up there telling these kiddies how to run the scout troop, and the next morning I was back in school being treated like a little kid.

In the fourth year he became a vice-prefect and enjoyed it. But those he was appointed to work with did not want elevation to full prefecthood: they had no 'interest in it'. To him:

Someone had given me a responsibility which no one had given me in school before. But simply by bad luck I was with two others who didn't care, with the result that the prefecting of my wing was very poor. The kids used to come in and muck about.

He was not elevated.

I was absolutely heartbroken.

It was as if this had been for him a final chance of being part of what was going on—of acquiring importance and prominence, and of becoming someone who might then be acknowledged. He says, tellingly:

For a little while I though maybe I should join in a bit more, I should justify it [his responsibility as a vice-prefect].

By that he meant considering at that point becoming someone who took school seriously and played an active part in it—trying out a different demeanour.

How I interpret Paul's story so far is this:

His first experience of secondary school had been of failure, despite his aberrant success in French. He had felt out of place; slightly ridiculous— with his 5 per cent in maths; and without hope of change for the better.

His failure was compounded by being taken away from this school, confirming all his feelings of inadequacy. But—like so many adolescents—he was an ambiguous creature. As well as carrying this certainty of having failed from his first school to his next, he was also robustly optimistic. Having met his adult equanimity, sturdiness, and sense of humour, I can imagine that this side of him was already in existence at an earlier stage. So, to begin with, things went well.

The work itself was reasonably easy . . . in most of the things I was at least up with them, if not ahead, so it gave me time to get used to it all.

By this he means becoming socially accepted by his peers—losing his northern accent, learning to support a local football team, acquiring the right protective colouring.

Robustly he succeeded. However, by the end of his first year at this second school (the end of his third year of secondary schooling), when he could relax and begin to take in what his teachers' attitudes to him were, he was disillusioned. His already strong—but temporarily stifled—feelings of inadequacy could surface again, confirmed by his teachers' failure to acknowledge what he felt himself to be—no longer a 'little kid'; and emphasized by what he took as their lack of interest in him.

An area of success

One teacher was different. Paul's one memory of success at this school is of his relationship with this teacher. Mr Franks appealed to him, so he decided to relinquish his disenchantment and try to make contact with him.

Courting Mr Franks, Paul had to make the first move. But he was capable of doing so. He was not someone who had lost most of his confidence, like David or Anne. He had enough belief in himself—even though he did not rate his ability very highly—to think it worth trying to attract Mr Franks's interest. He was demoralized; but not destroyed. He still believed that he was a person worthy of respect; and he felt that Mr Franks, at least, would respect him. His own words are: 'The teacher did care.'

Mr Franks taught maths. Despite the fact that Paul had thought himself almost innumerate at his previous school (remember his laughable 5 per cent), Mr Franks helped him eventually to succeed.

To begin with Paul was not specially acknowledged. He admired Mr Franks's thoroughness, from which he obviously gained; and I suspect that this teacher fought harder than most, and with more success, to reach all his pupils. But it is interesting that it was Paul's instinct to seek more: to seek acknowledgement. Being impressed by Mr Franks, and liking him, made him realize that this teacher's attention and acknowledgement were well worth acquiring. It was as if he knew that close and frequent contact with a teacher was what he needed, deserved, and was missing.

Because he was never terrorized, browbeaten, or afraid of bullying from his classmates—unlike Anne, who would at that stage have been incapable of imagining possible salvation from any teacher—he knew how to make Mr Franks notice him:

I used to go back occasionally after class—I'd never done that before—and do extra work; and he'd spend half an hour going over the stuff we'd done in the lesson. I found this very useful. Results were starting to improve.

During the summer holiday he gave me a load of test papers, and I wouldn't have done them for anybody else, but with him—I thought, this bloke's put in a lot of effort with me so I'm going to do it. I went through the lot. He couldn't believe it, and you could see him trying to hide his disbelief.

Paul forced himself out of anonymity and into a relationship with this maths teacher.

The moment after the summer holidays, when Mr Franks saw that Paul had done all the papers he had been given, could be said to be the best occasion of his secondary education. Perhaps what he saw on Mr Franks's face was not so much disbelief as pleasure.

Maths was one of the two O levels he passed.

Anne's revolution

Anne, in her thirties, was winkled slowly out of her lack of confidence by the teachers at her FE college.

After a while her handwriting deteriorated.

I was always very neat. Up till recently, coming here, my writing used to be extremely neat. It created a good impression—it didn't matter so much what you put in it. Partly it filled the time, and it looked nice.

Writing neatly and nicely had been one of her tactics to guarantee safety: her teachers could not criticize her for untidiness. Her writing could slide politely past her teachers' eyes without catching their attention. It is interesting, too, that 'neat writing' also offered a substitute, second-order satisfaction to someone whose education was giving her almost none. I asked her why she didn't write neatly now.

I think it is because I've gained in confidence, and I don't need to make it look so neat.

Paul gained confidence quickly when he went to the same FE college, straight from school. His words tell the story; and suggest what a fine place that college is:

I had a year here—and it's an easy thing to say, but I suppose it was about the best year I had ever had. It was certainly the most enjoyable to that date, and I think probably of the ones I've had, it was probably the best of all.

I asked him what made it so much better.

The relationships. I could wander in in the morning in whatever I chose to wear . . .

Mark the symbolism of that. He could choose to be himself: more grown up than his teachers at school had realized, dressed in clothes that he and not they had chosen.

I could talk to the teachers in a very adult way—not a teacher pretending you're an adult—but a more honest man-to-man basis.

They were great fun, they had dynamism, they cared about you, they were interested, they were good teachers, they could put their subject across, they were tremendous.

My educational experience had been disastrous up to then, basically, with one or two slight exceptions, and this year was so different.

The other people who'd come from school were basically like me, they weren't rebellious, they were my friends anyway, they were down-the-middle ones, and we met up with similar people from other schools. It just clicked. It just fell into place.

I had the most wonderful year.

He passed three more O levels.

Paul had been alienated at school because he had not been able to be what he felt himself to be; and his alienation went with a meagre theory of his own ability—though not so meagre, luckily, that he felt he couldn't gain from a year at college. But it was not until he had gained confidence from his success at work, that he began to look around at his friends with degrees, and estimate himself more soundly as someone likely to be just as gifted.

Let me briefly sum up these two accounts:

Anne, I think, lost nearly all sense of her own worth in school. Paul was luckier in that respect; he did not cease to believe in himself, though he did come to accept a far too low theory of his academic ability—as did Anne. Her position was worse: school, she felt, 'destroyed' her personality. But, different though their stories are, their evasive demeanour, their attempts to hide and present themselves as uninteresting, were remarkably similar. The same, too, is the fact that neither of their schools managed to see what their demeanour concealed.

The speed of Paul's 'recovery' shows how utterly his school had failed him—apart from his maths teacher. He was someone a school should have discovered and fostered and encouraged. He was entered for seven O levels and he passed only two. He was brimming with energy and talent, which his teachers failed to exploit. He was by nature an activist: a joiner, a leader, an instigator.

His story is an indictment of a school, and a demonstration of a school's capacity for failure. But how much worse an indictment is Anne's story: worse by the number of years more that she had to wait before her ability was discovered. Her school should have been able to perceive the sensitive and talented person her timid, evasive demeanour concealed; should have been able to take her neurotic anonymity as a warning.

With her, as with Paul, *disengagement*—prompted by very different reasons—*was accepted and not challenged.*

Judgements

How may teachers' judgements of Anne and of Paul have confirmed their neglect of these two talented people? For teachers, as I have said, have to judge in order to control, and in order to 'pitch' their teaching accurately. Teachers must at various times—despite, I suspect, thinking very little about them—have made decisions, however vague, about Anne and Paul.

Anne's early career in the second comprehensive she went to may have produced, for her teachers, several small glimpses of the ability that had to wait so long to be seen. There may, perhaps, have been an *unexpressed* consensus among them that she was—let's say—'quite a bright little girl'. But I suspect the 'judgement' that probably erased those glimpses day after day, was the result of the fact that she was very quiet and that her work was neither very good nor very bad.

So, though it is probable that she came to this school with a good report from an English teacher, at least, and was seen as someone with O level potential—day after day, the quality of her presence (or should I say absence?) and her uninteresting work, would have displaced any worthier, more optimistic assessment of her ability that might otherwise have been accepted. And the new, usurping, pessimistic, inadequate, hopelessly misrepresentative judgement might have gone something like this:

'Anne, yes, the one with the droopy long hair, tags around with those other two, what are their names? Yes, well, I don't think she's very bright—might get an O if she's lucky, but I doubt it. Does her work. Dull stuff, though. Doesn't give me any trouble. Nice little thing, really.'

Now, I think that when teachers judge pupils, *old evidence* stays fresh and commands attention when *new experience* keeps on validating it. So a pupil coming to School A, with a reputation from School B as a trouble-maker, who makes trouble from the start, will early on be judged as 'trouble'. If, thereafter, experience keeps on confirming this judgement, it will never waver. (Though an interesting aspect of this particular example is that to be labelled 'trouble' may determine that you produce trouble.)

When old evidence is startlingly contradicted by new experience, in the end the original judgement based on that old evidence may shift. So if a silent, average pupil suddenly becomes vocal and brilliant, she may then be judged to be more than average. (It has to be said, though, that teachers are often very reluctant indeed to acknowledge change—as if they do not like to be proved wrong. Certainty about their pupils may be so irretrievably important an element in their sense of security and control, that the admission of having got someone wrong may be a threat to that security.) In my first year at the Ashby Unit, David's performance as a lawyer did eventually force me to revise my judgement.

But when old evidence—and in Anne's case, remember, I am specu-lating that her good experience at her first secondary school may have handed over to the teachers at her second school a generous assessment of her potential—is only flickeringly or never corroborated by new experi-ence, *its power to determine judgement will fade and die,* particularly if the new experience is vague and indeterminate. Anne's teachers were given vague, modest, neat, unstartling work—the quality of which must have guaranteed that their reception of that work was itself vague. Such work does not encourage you as a teacher to think very hard or with any interest about its producer. When I marked Catherine's work, I am sure that I went on to automatic pilot. More of the same, I thought, slightly bored, uninterested in her uninteresting personality, as I had grown used to its vague presence in the Nomansland of her class.

I am therefore arguing that her teachers' experience of Anne—who guilefully and with fear made herself vague and elusive—was itself vague and inattentive. And the mist of vagueness generated by their vague relations would have blurred and finally concealed for good any *old* evidence of potential and talent. Thus would have been formed—in vagueness, inattention and boredom—the vague and misrepresentative judgement that I have just invented.

I prefer to think of this sort of obfuscating misrepresentation, born of vagueness out of ignorance, as unworthy of the word 'judgement', which suggests precision. Judgement of a pupil by teachers who acknowledge her in her uniqueness will be humble, open, provisional. It will be aware of *all* the evidence: that bequeathed from earlier schools; an anthology of teachers' hunches, past and present; the implications of particular pieces of work, and particular moments in lessons. It will, above all, be based on the truth that human biography is as full of discontinuity as continuity. It will say, 'this is what she's like, but she may change . . .'

However, the sort of statement teachers made about Anne was not judgement at all, but a sort of *running commentary*: a repetitious and inattentive response to uninteresting work and unremarkable presence.

Now for Paul. I would think it probable that Paul's teachers at his second secondary school did in the course of their commentaries remark on his earlier promise from time to time. He joined their school late; and early on he did fairly well. But he slid after less than a year, losing interest and hope, running his scout troop, and sick of being treated like a kid.

Commentaries thereafter would have gone something like this: 'Not doing a lot of work, keeps himself to himself, nice kid, gives me no trouble . . .'

Or they might have added: 'A little disappointing after his good start: needs to work harder.' Such a comment in a report would have been a pious gesture to his earlier promise: if he were to work harder, he might fulfil it. But, because on his own admission, he always did enough to 'get by', always did his just respectable modicum—while keeping himself scrupulously out of the limelight—they would not have translated such pieties into steady action. For a while, perhaps; but after a time, when nothing came of their attention, they would let him lollop along, comfortably, in the middle of the field, concentrating their excitement on those who might win, and those who were shying the fences or falling.

And gradually their commentaries might have begun to suggest: 'He's not really as good as we thought . . .' Again, the point would have been that the very vagueness of their experience of him guaranteed obfuscation of a more generous assessment of his worth.

Old evidence, then, only continues to dictate perception if new experience maintains its relevance. This is one of the keys to understanding the predicament of the lost and misapprehended.

Relegation

This word is important to my argument. Those who taught Anne and Paul colluded with their evasions and their self-dreprecation, and relegated them to neglect in Nomansland. I did the same with John.

I taught John first in his and my first year, when he seemed intelligent and lively; which is why, I think, I also remember him at a later stage, when I was teaching him to pass his Higher in English. By then he was tall, good-looking, strongly built—no longer a small boy who seemed to laugh readily and act quickly. He had become slow, lethargic, bored. I suspect that at this stage he was very like Paul at the same point in his school career: that he had become disenchanted.

Having had nothing to do with him in the intervening years, I could remember what he had been like a long time before; and I did my best to make contact with him. But he did not respond. He was pleasant enough, sitting there quietly; writing, if asked, just enough to escape rebuke; doing his homework eventually, though never very well.

He was in a big class: twenty-seven. Circumstances were against my doing much for him. There were plenty who were interested and busy; and others who were quite interested and quite busy, but whose work was erratic and who cried out for my guidance. There were even some who made my work difficult by talking too much.

And you can't succeed with all: you can't get all your pupils to pass. Oddly, the credential hunt, though it makes teachers sniff out success, also makes them accept failure. The hunt is charged with competitiveness: and it's a law of competition that some have to lose.

I made up my mind early on that John would be a loser: and we got on genially enough thereafter. I took it for granted there was little I could do, and left him to his own devices.

In a sense I was right. In distributing my scant time, some had to go short, so I relegated him and probably five or six others to the region where my attention went not; or not very often, and not for very long when it did.

He gave me no trouble, and so could be relegated with ease. After a while my earlier feelings about him—my old evidence—faded, while a new judgement tailored itself from my daily experience of his disenchantment: 'He's not really very bright . . .'

There was no *good* reason for believing that this was the case.

CHAPTER FOUR

How his teachers relegated Roger

IT should be no surprise that 'judgement' is becoming a central theme of this book. Whether you believe in psychoanalysis or in a less mysterious psychology, it must be hard to dispute what I take to be the fact of our tendency to internalize judgements made of us.

How freely and frequently schools and teachers judge. It is their neutral, uninterested judgements—their inattentive running commentaries—that are internalized by the inhabitants of Nomansland.

Suppose that most who find themselves there test out theories of their mediocrity. 'I'm not much good', was Anne's thought when she arrived at college in her thirties. 'I might just be up to an O level or two.' This was the theory she had begun to test when, at school, she had asked no questions, done little work, and avoided her teachers' attention. Her successful evasion guaranteed her teachers' inattentiveness and their meagre judgements; just as John's bored passivity guaranteed his relegation as 'not much good'. And her teachers' inattentiveness taught Anne a great deal.

If 'testing theories' is a helpful way of suggesting how the adolescent pieces together an identity, then inattentiveness and relegation are the proof that someone like Anne needs in order to accept her theory. Her self-belittlement was proved correct.

The irony is that teachers—seeing the passive faces of their quietest, most biddable pupils—accept them as decent citizens in the making. But their passivity may be nothing but timid experiment.

In many ways, judging is the teacher's crucial act. It is what gives the teacher professional pride. One way of putting this would be to say that schools exist to process children, to send them out, appropriately accredited, into different walks of life. The divisions of society are maintained by this process; so that when a teacher judges a pupil, he is acting out a role which society expects of him.

Constraints, pressures, his isolation as one adult among many children, the credentialist system: all these urge the teacher to judge. But this great social expectation may produce the keenest pressure of all.

How an adolescent interprets the judgements that surround him will determine his theories of his worth and ability. But some of these judgements may be vague and ill-founded, however conclusively pronounced. Definitely conclusive may be the doubts, fears and lapses of self-esteem these judgements prompt—feelings which act as theories, in their power to determine demeanour and academic performance.

A teacher is likely to be a 'significant other': one whose reactions, assessment, acclamations, and judgements are received by pupils in such a way as to affect, confirm, or change what they are and what they do. When a teacher arrives at a judgement, she may be helping to determine a pupil's future: may be giving a pupil experimental evidence with which to turn a theory into his own firm self-judgement.

At best, when teacher and pupil acknowledge each other, such negotiation is accurate, subtle, inclusive, optimistic, sympathetic. But at worst we are dealing with judgements made in the dark *of* judgements made in the dark.

Roger the stubborn enigma

My first impression of Roger was of someone very cautious, not easily hoodwinked or browbeaten or astonished. He was big, good-looking, and strongly built, with thick dark hair. He spoke in a quiet, unemphatic voice, in the accent of the area where he was brought up—though his parents came from far away, in the West Country. From the outset, I sensed watchful, considerable intelligence.

We were soon talking about *his* idea of his gifts. He was at David's FE college to take three more O levels to add to the three he had achieved at school. He told me that he could only do O levels, he could never do A levels.

I nagged at this idea. 'How do you know?' I asked.

'I think they're too far ahead of me,' he replied.

'What makes you think that?' I wanted to know.

'Well, A levels you always associate with people who get lots of O levels in school.'

I argued with this on the grounds that it might in many cases be true, but was not necessarily so; and finished by saying, 'I think it's interesting that you've got a firm idea of your limitations without actually knowing what your limitations are.'

'I think they would be my limitations.'

'Yes, but you don't know, do you?'

I could say this with some confidence, because he had admitted that he never did any work—and so had never really tested himself. But he had picked up three O levels just the same—which, I suggested, might be a sign of considerable intelligence.

I suspected that Roger's theory of his ability was based on some very flimsy evidence indeed. I was fascinated by the specious circularity of: 'People who get A levels are those who get lots of O levels. I did not get lots of O levels, therefore I am not the sort of person to get A levels.' This was a fair comment on the usual pattern of school success; but a less than accurate judgement of his own worth was probably implied.

We established that by his third year he was someone for whom, like Paul, school had begun to mean rather little. The good bits of life were outside school: football, and Heavy Metal, and his mates who had been his mates since primary school.

I also discovered that his thoughts about A levels were partly based on a phantasy of the 'brilliant scholar'. This evil creature fogs so many people's clarity when they try to come to a fair judgement of their abilities. I had a phantasy of the brilliant scholar embodied in a classmate called Peter. When we were doing a 'timed essay', he would look at the question written on the blackboard—which we were to answer in forty minutes—for a few seconds. Then he would unscrew his old-fashioned pen and begin to write. After forty minutes, three or four pages would be covered in his neat handwriting. There would be no crossings-out. He would screw up his pen again, look quizzically around at the rest of us, and at me—as likely as not by then to be chewing my pen in desperation, with nothing on paper at all. His essays were always good ones, and he seemed to do no work for them.

Paul had his brilliant scholar too: his friend who never did any work, and went to Oxford. His descriptions suggest that this friend went to school, yawning and disdainful, already with nothing to learn from his teachers, and left for Oxford after no exertion.

This is Roger's phantasy. It comes after a telling description of the depth of his disenchantment:

You just strolled along to lessons, did what you did and went. You never seem to think of the exam till it's right on top of you, about a month before, and you suddenly realize all this stuff you've been doing, you haven't been taking any notice, you've just been doing it, and then you end up with a month, and seven subjects to try to crawl through—and if you can do it then you do it, and if you can't then you fail, and it's been a whole waste of time. I think there are a very few kids who actually go through thinking about the exams from the beginning.

Who were they, I wanted to know.

The very intelligent ones who find it easy, and they'll fly through the exams, and they start revising very early, before you've even thought about the exams.

So he judged himself by reference to his failure to be up with the 'very intelligent ones'.

In our second interview, I asked him to explore this further.

I've never considered myself to be intelligent because people I consider to be intelligent have A levels, and I'm saying that I can't do A levels. When I was in the first and second years, even O levels seemed impossible to me.

What was his evidence for that, I asked.

There wasn't any really, they just seemed to be something for the really bright kids.

That suggested that as far as he was concerned, he wasn't one of them. How had he got that conviction into his head?

I don't know, it's just something you feel that you can't do.

What was it to do with?

Well, my friends who are intelligent, who are a lot more intelligent than me, they're the ones who are going to do A levels. Paul, for example, he doesn't look it, he looks pretty docile, but he's got about five O levels and he's doing A's now.

What showed his intelligence?

He was so clever and so fast in lessons. He'd have answers off the top of his head. He knew he could go out and get A levels.

He added:

His house looks middle-class, his father's in business.

I wondered to what extent Roger's stubborn convictions about O and A levels were an expression of the fact that he did not feel 'middle-class'.

In classes he slumped, bored for the most part—except in maths and history; though even in those subjects he did not do much work because he had always found them easy to 'pick up'. He was a victim of the dreary secondary school diet of working for exams, never for now— never for interest, for the zest of solving problems, for the pleasure of using his brain. So many stories I listened to were mournfully redolent of this dreariness: the prevailing weather of Nomansland.

Roger's parents

Roger's parents found Roger baffling. I interviewed them both together. Roger's father, a forceful, bright man, a welder who had left school early and wanted Roger to achieve what he hadn't been able to, said:

Sometimes when you're explaining things to him he'll cut across you and put you exactly where you should be, and you'll think, Christ, he's right, he's seen through that. He's cut through all the drivel and the extraneous material, and he says something, and you think, why couldn't I have thought of that?

At primary school, Roger had been seen as bright; though even at that stage, towards the end, he was seen as a coaster, as someone who wouldn't push himself. His parents were frustrated by him, certain he had more ability than he thought, more than his own expectations suggested. Their judgement was different from his, and based on intuitions arising from their intimate knowledge of him. They could point to his contemptuous dismissal of inessentials, and say, 'That shows his intelligence.' His mother said:

There's no wasting words. He can describe something exactly.

Their judgement of his intelligence was not categorical, but speculative. They based it on their own feelings; though they also made use of the comments and judgements of his teachers at primary school. And like all judgement based on acknowledgement, theirs was open, optimistic, subtle, and inclusive.

Mother: The deputy head who he had at his last primary school thought he'd do all right academically. But he said, he does tend to do just enough, and this is what we've had ever since.

Father: Which to my mind shows he is intelligent, to know enough to know what he's got to do.

Their interpretation of his passivity, his caution—his low profile—is subtle and speculative. At his second primary school, aged 7, Roger was suddenly in a much larger school where he knew no one, having moved from a small school in a rural area. His younger brother began school shortly afterwards, and, being slightly disabled, attracted a certain amount of bullying. So Roger defended him. His parents think that the sudden change, and the predicament of his younger brother, made

Roger see school as a hostile place in which he must learn, cleverly, to survive. They also feel that when he went to his comprehensive school, he was frightened of expecting too much of himself: that he saw high expectations as themselves hostile, bullying, leading to intolerable demands and pressures.

His father suspects that he may have contributed by putting on too much pressure: saying work hard, get your qualifications, or you'll end up like me, with nothing. And I suspect that Roger, respecting his father, found it impossible to want to be altogether different.

His parents also recognized something enigmatic about him, which they took as slightly awesome; a sign, if anything, of his intelligence. They knew he had 'something up his sleeve' in the way of an ambition: something he wanted to do in life. But he wasn't going to tell them; and they respected his reticence.

What his teachers thought

To find out what Roger's teachers thought, I wrote to his history teacher, Mrs Roberts, and asked for an interview. She very kindly agreed. As so often with teachers who helped me with my research, she did so out of interest in my subject, which I had explained at length in my letter. Roger had suggested that I contact her, because, he said, he 'quite liked her', and because history had been one of his 'good' subjects.

I interviewed her in an empty classroom, somehow well fitted to our task. We sat near the front of about six lines of desks, adding up to about thirty in all. The ghosts of large classes were palpably present in the room.

I took to Mrs Roberts—as to most of the teachers I interviewed. It was rare not to be impressed by their eagerness to talk about their work; their impatience with the constraints put upon them; their obvious pride in the importance of what they were doing. Mrs Roberts had gone to a great deal of trouble—talking to a number of Roger's teachers to ask them what they had thought of him; trying to analyse her own impressions; preparing herself to help me. Like all teachers, she had very little time to spare for such work.

She told me that Roger had not made a very deep impression on her. She was not even sure whether or not she had taught him earlier than the fourth year, when he was in her history class.

She found him, she said, mildly irritating, though on the whole she left him to his own devices. He contributed little to lessons, and never did much work. Sometimes, though not often, he would rather lazily join more active classmates in mild disruption.

She recalled parents' evenings, when Roger would promise his father to work harder:

But you could see he was fairly obstinate and that it was water off a duck's back; he'd heard it before and he'd hear it again. He'd sit there and go, yes, no, because it was the easiest thing for him to do.

Whereas she would tell his father:

He is lazy, he day-dreams, and if he can sit and chat instead of work, he will.

His chatting, she made clear, was the discreet, barely audible, sort that was not very disruptive.

Three things, I assume, pressed Mrs Roberts to try to get Roger to work harder. First, her own considerable professional pride: she was the sort of teacher who would want her pupils to do as well as possible. Second, her need for good results to maintain her reputation: she had not yet taught many 'exam classes'. And third, she also, it seemed, had a suspicion that Roger did have some ability:

Roger did show a couple of sparks of knowing what was going on . . .

He showed his—rare—sparks in discussions; but for most of the time he did too little and took no active part in lessons.

Now, as I have suggested, Roger's own hypothesis of his ability was well worked out and firm. Reading his reports from earlier in his school career, it seems that his passivity—or 'laziness' as many called it—had a long history; and that *certainty* about himself—that he was not 'academic'—had also appeared very early in his career.

A primary teacher, for instance, criticized, in a bizarre phrase to describe a 10 year-old, his 'superior attitude' to his work, and expressed irritation at his failure to realize that more industry was necessary. It's as if he judged, even then, that it was not worthwhile to commit himself to doing much work.

Mrs Roberts, too, met not only his passivity, but also this certainty: the brick wall of his refusal to respond to exhortation. She says that she increased her exhortations after parents' evenings, but that:

He probably got ignored to a great extent. Except perhaps after parents' evenings— when you think—right, Roger, I'm going to go on at you, and you go on at him for a couple of weeks and you don't get any results, *so you give up and go on to those you do get results from*.

In other words—my words—she relegated him.

Mrs Roberts reported on a discussion she had with two colleagues:

I couldn't really work out whether I thought Roger was intelligent or not, and that's why I went to Jen, his English teacher [who had taught Roger for longer] and Mr Mynors who had directed Roger in the fifth-year play. We all said, well perhaps Roger *is* intelligent.

Then Jen said, no, I don't think he is intelligent; and we were dancing round the subject.

I strongly suspect that such a conversation about Roger had not taken place before. It is interesting that, given what may well have been their first opportunity to think about Roger, to focus on him, their first reaction was doubt. This, I think, is probably typical of what most teachers would think, feel, and say were they given the opportunity to consider their inhabitants of Nomansland. Doubt expressed the inadequacy of these teachers' evidence about Roger, the infrequency of their encounters with him, the imprecision of their thoughts about him. Even when they focused, what they saw was blurred.

But teachers do not like doubt. These three wanted to decide what they thought: certainty at all costs:

We came to the conclusion that he was probably rightly placed when he was in the second group for English and not the top group. We don't think he is exceptionally intelligent. He's the sort of child who could perhaps cope with a few O levels . . .

Mrs Roberts said later that if Roger had worked hard all year, he might have attained a B pass in history, but would never have achieved an A.

Here, then, we have a beautiful example of 'categorical certainty' combined with doubt and vagueness; a sense of glimpses and impressions blurred, unresolved, and undeveloped—combined with clear, definitive statements about his ability.

Under pressure from her two colleagues, who suggested tentatively that Roger might have underachieved, Jen became very defensive, and suggested that her estimate of his ability should have been lower:

She got very 'I did my best for him'. She reckoned that for him to have got his C pass in English was very good.

I suspect that she sensed the fallibility, the inadequacy, of what had gone on between her and Roger; but instead of examining this sensation, she decided that her teaching had been successful, and that he was lucky to have done as well as he did.

This, I suggest, is an example of a teacher not wanting to admit that it is not always possible to reach all pupils and teach them with equal success. Rather than admit this, and that Roger had eluded her, she defined him with almost vindictive precision, totally at variance with the doubt that surfaced in the first part of the conversation between these three teachers.

Of course she knew what he was all about. She taught all her pupils as individuals, didn't she, and saw and understood them all equally? I sensed a twinge of guilt, from a teacher burdened with the impossible expectation that she should arrange the fulfilment of all her pupils.

Mrs Roberts seems to have been more concerned with Roger's 'laziness' and unresponsiveness than with her suspicion of his ability. She tried to get him to work; he wouldn't; so she was presented with a problem.

The problem was how to explain his unresponsiveness and how to justify her relegation of him: her acceptance of him as the sort of person who wouldn't get more than a few O levels. (Though at another point she suggested he might be capable of 'one A level going on two if he had a good day'—which implies that the ability she sniffed was a great deal higher than she admitted in *most* of what she said. It implies too that her need to justify his relegation must have been all the keener.)

She had to justify her decision that he belonged out of range of her attention; that he should be *ignored to a great extent*.

Relegation justified

All teachers want to reach all their pupils—as Jen wanted, and probably failed to do in Roger's case. They do not *want* to relegate anyone, especially a pupil who shows 'sparks'. But what can they do, when many of the others seem willing to work, except leave someone like Roger to his own devices?

Because Mrs Roberts was a hard-working, dedicated teacher who believed that she should succeed with all her pupils, she felt guilty when Roger eluded her. In order to deal with this guilt in such a way that it would not interfere with her competence and her professional self-esteem, she decided that there was nothing she could have done; not because it *is* impossible to reach all your pupils (that way madness lies: the revelation that the job asked is nearly impossible), but because Roger himself was at fault:

the general impression we came out with, most of all, is that he does not like external authority. He didn't like being told what to do.

Nothing she could have done would have made any difference, because he was fixed in a psychological impasse in which he could not respond positively to her exhortations.

Thus was she let off the hook; and thus in a real, not speculative, case can we see how a teacher's judgement can confirm a pupil's membership of Nomansland.

It is important to be clear that the judgement Mrs Roberts provided herself with is an *explanation* of Roger's unresponsiveness; and a very inadequate one. No one who has worked with adolescents would deny that many find it difficult to recognize authority. But generally this difficulty has a meaning, is for detailed and discoverable reasons. In this case, Roger's opposition was partly from boredom, but mainly from his own certainty about his limited abilities. There was no point in responding and doing masses of work, because he knew it would lead nowhere. But instead of finding out such things, Mrs Roberts, like Jen, relegated Roger, and defined him in such a way as to justify her relegation.

It is interesting that her definition was psychological in origin. A little psychology is a dangerous thing; and teachers seldom have more than a little. The idea that 'he does not like external authority' represents any sort of adequate explanation of anything is absurd: you are no further forward in *understanding* someone's behaviour, if you say such a thing, until you ask 'why?' and try to come up with some answers.

Mrs Roberts was not trying to understand Roger; she was trying to relegate him comfortably, so that he could be *ignored to a great extent*. She backed up her general explanation—held up as particular and incontestable—with more handy psychology. Not only does she attribute a psychological failing to him—dislike of authority—but she also decides that he is developmentally a laggard:

I just got the general impression, immaturity; Roger, please grow up. My impression was that he was immature—right the way through.

So—she's got him cut and dried. I mean her no disrespect when I say that there is a slightly vindictive quality to her justification of his relegation. He's 'lazy', he 'dislikes authority', he's 'immature'.

What she means by this last frequently-heard word is: 'Roger does not respond to my exhortations. A sensible, grown-up boy would see the sense of responding to me. Roger doesn't. So Roger cannot be grown up.' This is a logically leaky sequence of thought; and in my experience, 'immature' is generally used by teachers as a handy way of accounting for failure. It is a word ideally suited for the sort of relegation I am describing: there was nothing she could do to force Roger to grow up; so she was free to attend to the needs of those who *were* grown up enough to respond to her teaching.

There are other comforting sources of pseudo-explanation, the best known being 'domestic pathology'. A disruptive or difficult pupil is often the beneficiary of enormous amounts of time devoted to trying to help her to change, to 'improve'; but as soon as teachers give up on such a pupil, you will hear them all muttering, 'What can you expect with a home like hers?'

A late-flowering relationship

What, above all, did not develop between Roger and Mrs Roberts was a proper relationship based on acknowledgement. Interestingly, Mrs Roberts said:

I never really worked out whether I liked him or disliked him.

This I take to mean that she had not made a relationship with him which allowed her to know what he was, what made him tick. It is a statement that bespeaks the great vagueness of her feelings about him.

But he still got his C pass in her subject. He looked into school after he had left. He found Mrs Roberts and said hello to her. Her head of department was in the room, and he asked Roger, 'Aren't you going to thank Mrs Roberts for your O level?' (I could add here the snide aside that when pupils fail, it's their fault, but when they succeed, it's the teacher's fault.)

And he went on—yes, well, thank you Mrs Roberts, and after that he and another boy—another unexpected O level—within the week had sent me a tape with some music on it. He'd found out that I was into heavy music, and he'd made up a selection of his favourite pieces and sent them to me.

Was that a surprise, I asked.

Yes, it was, I was highly delighted; and he'd written a little letter with it to say thank you very much, so I was quite touched.

I've seen him once or twice since then and he's very much more mature.

I shall return soon to the implications of that last fascinating statement.

The irony of this development is keen: too late does Roger become approachable; or, rather, too late does he approach. Too late does he do something successful which wins the attention and interest of his teacher, and some credit for her too. Too late does he begin to behave towards her as if she were a human being, with similar musical tastes to his own. Too late begins the flowering of a relationship between them— if that is not too elaborate a way of putting it.

Who knows what different judgements of his ability might have been made, by both Roger and Mrs Roberts, if they had begun to relate to each other earlier on? For it is *certain* that no one, neither his teachers nor he himself, knows what his abilities really are.

The conversation Mrs Roberts reported shows how uncertain his teachers were about his gifts; but instead of celebrating their uncertainty as proof of his interesting and enigmatic nature—and trying to find out more about him—they opted for 'just above average' as an adequate description of him, and thought no more about him.

What else could they have done? They could have tried to get to know him, tried to excite him, tried to engage him. But he, determined that he was not academic, obstinately bored, and almost deliberately disenchanted, was not easily to be won over.

But I suspect that something had in fact begun to change in their attitude and approach to him before he left school, which suggests the beginnings of one answer to the question I have just asked. The late flowering of the relationship between Roger and Mrs Roberts had already begun, before he left school.

He was in the fifth-year play. He had not been in a production before.

We gave him the part of an over-confident doctor who wouldn't be told what to do and always got things wrong; and he fitted into that part superbly, and no direction was needed, and he really had a very good time. And he really did start to flourish, this last couple of weeks in the term.

After explaining this, Mrs Roberts reiterated her point about Roger's immaturity; and then said, disarmingly, that she and her colleagues had tried to get him to grow up and work all through his schooling:

And he didn't do this until his last two weeks.

In their helplessness to do much to hook the recalcitrant, teachers have to leave the responsibility for change to them, have to wait for them to do the right thing, to 'grow up', to see the light. Similarly, as I have said, when their attempts to make contact do fail, they attribute deficiencies to their pupils in order to explain this failure.

Therefore, Mrs Roberts, happy with her explanation of Roger's recalcitrance as being from dislike of authority, and immaturity, is forced to explain his blossoming in the school play as being from sudden miraculous loss of these deficiencies.

What was undoubtedly beginning to take place was an abrupt change in the quality of Roger's school life. He was doing something, for the first time in secondary school, which he really enjoyed, and in which he was a success. Committed and interested, of course he seemed different from the boy teachers were used to in class, with his faultless torpor and his dogged disengagement; and of course they began, tentatively, to get to know him and relate to him.

But Mrs Roberts preferred the miraculous as explanation:

I saw him in the staffroom when I was running around between scenes, and he'd plonked himself down on a sofa with his feet up, and I thought he was an adult.

He'd grown as well, physically. He was quite small and dumpy for a long time. And in the fourth year he was quite tall. But—I don't know—everything seemed to go during those last two weeks: his physical stature, the rest—you know.

I had to look twice to make sure it was Roger.

This seems to me the most wonderful description of a teacher's sudden release from preconception that I could have found.

There is no doubt that a relationship began to develop between them as her relegating judgement faded:

And during the fifth-year party after the play, I was surprised by how much attention he gave me. He came down and sat with me—and I never thought we'd really connected.

They hadn't—in class.

Had this experience taken place two years before, it is likely that Roger's relationship with Mrs Roberts would have been very different. Instead of simply hearing and recording Roger's few sparks, she would have pounced fiercely on them, pressed him for more; kept him behind after lessons to tell him what an intelligent comment he had made; suggested books for him to read and television programmes for him to watch. Instead of which Roger had to wait until he was leaving to begin to be *acknowledged*.

The moments when he showed his sparks were not only moments when he showed his ability—but moments when two people approached and almost acknowledged each other; when Roger said, in effect, 'you are interesting: look, you have made me think'; and Mrs Roberts said, 'that was an interesting thing to say'; when, had they led to more such exchanges, the relationship that had to wait so long to develop might have begun; when Roger took sorties into friendly territory—but then went back to Nomansland.

Changing theories, or having them changed

Adolescents base their expectations of themselves, and design their demeanour, according to theories about their nature and ability. Both expectations and demeanour are experiment to test those theories. So if pupils manipulate teachers into accepting their first tentative hypotheses about themselves—into judging them as, experimentally, they are presenting themselves—they may take that acceptance as good enough proof of the accuracy of those hypotheses. Unless the pupils themselves change those hypotheses, or something else changes them, they are likely to become immutable.

The most dangerous hypothesis to test in school is that you are not very able, not very attractive, not very interesting. It is dangerous, because you will present yourself, experimentally, as dull, vague, and uninteresting. If your choice of this hypothesis accompanies, or is the result of, fear of other people, your experimental dullness and vagueness will have a defensive power that will make it unusually consistent.

If you show your dullness and vagueness to teachers in class—a setting which is both the source of your fear and the laboratory for your experiment—that dullness and vagueness will guarantee your teachers' inattention; and your hypothesis will be confirmed.

If the way you test your hypothesis is by evasion and camouflage, teachers will not look at you closely enough to discover whether what you seem is what you are. Trained and expected to judge and to judge quickly, they will assume that they do know you.

If a teacher looks at you more closely, he may find evidence inconsistent with your theory, and challenge it. When an adolescent experiments to test one theory, he is probably at the same time repressing another: adolescence is the time of life of most ambiguity. If a teacher looks closely enough, he may winkle out the temporarily abandoned idea, and work to confirm it. So Paul, without—I think—knowing quite why he was doing so, approached his excellent maths teacher, and won from him corroboration of his abandoned idea that he was capable after all of academic achievement. The maths teacher acknowledged him; and perhaps began the resurrection of confidence that ended at FE college with Paul's Great Leap Forward.

Paul's was an example of a 'pupil changing his theory'. For he must, in some degree, have been saying to himself, 'It's worth a try, maybe I'll make it with this man. Maybe I'm okay at maths after all—not just someone who used to score 5 per cent in the exam and make everyone laugh.'

But Roger was not going to change his hypothesis himself: he was quite happy with his own estimate of his ability. For that to change, he was dependent on being acknowledged by a teacher who could challenge that acceptance. In *class* his bored disengagement protected him from teachers' attention and guaranteed that they would not acknowledge him; and, unlike Paul, there was nothing in him that wanted to reverse that low estimate.

The first inklings of acknowledgement occurred when he was seen and appreciated outside the classroom, in a setting in which his modest idea of his abilities was irrelevant—so need not affect the way he showed himself. The play appealed to him. He enjoyed himself. He began to like Mrs Roberts, and she to like him. That liking, had it begun earlier, might have led to full acknowledgement and a challenge to his theories about himself.

She, and the other teachers working on the play, seeing him forthcoming, exuberant, engaged, intelligent, would have offered him a route out of Nomansland. They would not thereafter have been content with his passivity in class. Their sense of his intelligence in another setting would have given them energy to seek him out. Doing this from a starting point of positive feelings reciprocated by Roger would have allowed a chance of shaking his rigidly convinced theories about himself and his abilities.

But his first experience of acting came too late.

It is interesting that Roger was eventually discovered by Mrs Roberts and upgraded to maturity in a setting the purpose of which was *play*. His excitement when given an opportunity to play at being someone else implies how asphyxiating had been the constraint of his self-belittlement in class. Acting, he could breathe more freely, could stretch, seemed taller and larger and more intelligent.

Seeing pupils in as many different circumstances as possible is a good idea, because it adds to the available evidence about them. The greater the amount of evidence, the lesser the scope for misjudgement. Seeing him only in class—where his meagre convictions determined the little he showed of himself—Mrs Roberts's understanding of Roger was over-simplified. Simplification of those in Nomansland is the theme of my next chapter.

CHAPTER FIVE

The over-simplification of Jane

IF I tried to identify the most important characteristic of their schooling shared by all the witnesses I have called so far, it would be that teachers did not acknowledge them. But it was their silence and evasiveness that prevented teachers from approaching them. It is difficult to acknowledge a pupil who seldom speaks or returns your gaze.

Teachers do not worry about the silent and evasive. Instead, silence and evasiveness generate in teachers' reactions and judgements that fatal alloy of vagueness and spurious certainty.

Such judgements, above all, over-simplify, and neglect complexity.

Jane

Jane was not at the FE college where I found so many to interview. She is a friend of mine. I knew her first as a darts player in the pub I used to go to when I first worked at the Ashby Unit, and I took to her partly because of an enigmatic quality I wanted to fathom.

Sometimes she would be very quiet, and smile only moderately, cautiously, in conversation. At such times she could look almost grey with neutrality, all colour gone from her face. She could look strained, depressed, anxious. But I would never be tempted to intrude, to try to draw her into conversation, to cheer her up. She always seemed strong, self-sufficient. Even her neutrality, her withdrawal seemed deliberate, definite.

At other times she would come into the pub talkative, quick in conversation to cap remarks, to laugh, to join in. At these times her intelligence was vivid; and she would look quite different. Her cheeks would have colour in them, she would no longer look strained and anxious—but slim and elegant. Her smile would be beautiful—all the more for its sudden arrival.

I cannot remember now how it was that I sought to interview her, and found out that her school career was likely to be interesting. She was at that time working as a clerk, and I think my first glimmer of interest was to find out what sort of education had led someone so intelligent into this walk of life.

Jane's story follows Anne's and David's very closely. It seems that large numbers of people go to school, find some of its demands too much to deal with—and retire to Nomansland. The particular reasons for the reaction of each of them will be different, distinct. But the demeanour they adopt, and the strategy for coping and avoidance they employ, tend to be remarkably similar.

Perhaps it is best to see Jane as someone predisposed from very early on to seek anonymity, not to make herself stand out. At primary school, she says, she never played a large part in lessons, did not join in. At 9, she went to her middle school. There, talk of exams and their importance began very early. It is as if the change to a bigger school, where she had to wear a uniform for the first time, coincided with a douche of reality. Play—she recalls primary school as a time of play—was now over, and the real world was to begin to claim her:

All of a sudden we were made to work.

She worked well at her middle school; and in science subjects she was particularly successful. She was always 'near the top'. She loved the lessons. She liked the teacher, and still sees her from time to time:

I found her interesting and could listen to her. I tried very hard. I got on well with her.

We had already established that Jane said little in class, tended to hold her peace. So I asked her if she behaved differently in the science teacher's classes.

I was more attentive and more willing to ask questions.

But she would always let herself down in exams. She would:

go to pieces. I'd just sometimes sit there and be blank. Because my mind wouldn't work, it would freeze.

Her failure would be moderate; she would always do just well enough to escape attention; to earn 'a disappointing exam' rather than an enquiry into the difference between the quality of her term's work and her exam result.

It seems, then, that her fear of exams, and hatred of them, began very early. And her pattern of good work in the term—or reasonably good work—followed by exam disappointment, continued when she went to her comprehensive senior school.

She was placed in 'a high stream'; and for her first year (two years before her O level year) it was still thought that she would probably be an O level candidate. The quality of some of the work she was producing —though she says that by her second and third years (aged 15 and 16) she was doing less and less—must have kept some idea of her ability alive, to judge by the reports written about her at the beginning of her third year. But she did not speak, did not ask questions or in any way make herself prominent. She did not encourage her teachers to be interested in her, or in her difficulties with exams.

At the beginning of her third year, a choice had to be made as to whether she would take O level or CSE. And in those same reports we can sense her teachers' ignorance of her; and we can see, very clearly, the process of relegation at work. They state, again and again, one term before the final decision was made, that Jane will not be put in for O level but for CSE instead. In many schools, pupils were not sorted out into O or CSE candidates until this late stage, and the threat of demotion was used as a spur to industry. In Jane's case, they said, it was her failure to work hard enough that necessitated her demotion; failure alone was justification enough, and it was not examined.

Her history teacher said:

Jane's work has shown little effort this term and I cannot possibly enter her for the O level exam.

Note the familiar tone of relegation: disappointment, disgruntlement, and a slight touch of vindictiveness. Her biology teacher said:

A pass at O level would need a tremendous amount of hard work, she might be advised to sit CSE.

and her maths teacher:

Plenty of careful revision *may* lead to some improvement.

They don't mention her ability—though the suggestion that if she worked she would manage O level implies that they thought she was able. But perhaps the lack of direct mention suggests that their notion of her ability was fading fast as time went on and she showed no sign of working hard enough.

What, however, is certain, is that Jane's teachers did not try to find out why she wasn't working hard enough; why she always flunked exams and tests.

I asked her why she thought her teachers did not try to find out what was wrong.

Because I sat at the back not doing anything. I didn't show myself and say LOOK I want you to find out about me.

Some went beyond relegation to rejection. She tended to chat discreetly to her friends:

. . . idle chatter [her chemistry teacher called it]. A CSE entry would be advisable.

One teacher does, however, at least sniff enigma, complexity:

Jane seems such a sensible girl in the form [said her form tutor] that it is disappointing to find out that she does not extend that good sense sufficiently to her work. We expect some improvement!

It was up to Jane, of course, to provide that improvement.

For an enigma to niggle sufficiently to attract thought or action, it must be far more noticeable, far more maddening; or the disparity between past ability and present failure must be glaring, and far greater than in Jane's case.

Jane was clear about the sort of pupils who would have earned that sort of attention:

only those kids who were really difficult, naughty, *if* they were quite bright. They'd be taken to one side and given a quiet chat.

But Jane did not earn that sort of attention. She was consistently frightened of exams and consistently failed to do well in them. After a while she gave up trying, so certain was she of failure. She admits 'denial' here: that she compensated for her difficulty by pretending that it wasn't important. Exams were just bits of paper; people would have to judge her for what she was, she decided. But at the same time, when, the year before, her science teacher—looking at her poor exam result—said she hadn't done enough work, she was angry, because she knew that she had. I asked if she expressed that anger. 'No.'

That was the trouble. She didn't say anything about her difficulties or her feelings, and because she didn't make them obvious, her teachers neither noticed nor suspected them. Her denial was so successful that she presented herself, misleadingly, as a cheerful enough pupil, with her interests elsewhere: lazy, agreeable, well-behaved, quiet.

I imagine that, just as on her 'grey' days, she comes across as someone strong, not to be invaded by cheery offers of friendliness, so did she appear to her teachers as someone who had made a firm and definite decision to opt out. She would have appeared happy to have done so, and perfectly self-sufficient. But this was a façade, dictated by her pride: the last thing she wanted was for her teachers to guess her feelings of failure and inadequacy. Adolescents are very clever at disguising such feelings, and it is often of utmost importance to them to do so.

Seeing someone strong and well-behaved, but not hard-working; pleasant, but not assiduous, her teachers must have been annoyed.

Jane seems such a sensible girl . . .

So why can't she put her good sense to better use? Sensible, pleasant girls are normally hard workers.

We expect some improvement!

This comment shows a teacher depending on her recalcitrant pupil to do her changing unaided. 'We expect some improvement' is a magnificently disinterested (the girl is really nothing to do with me) gesture of dissociation.

The reason that this teacher can thus wash her hands is that Jane did *enough work* to get by; was not going to be a catastrophic and embarrassing flop; was going, after all, to get some decent CSEs. Let it not be forgotten, too, that the fact that she was pleasant and quiet meant that they could leave her to her own devices—to pull her socks up unaided—and so have more time to spend on more pressing problems and more interesting pupils.

I need hardly add, that Jane had no particular relationship with a teacher: she was not special for any one of them. A familiar story; she made insufficient impact to attract enquiry, doubt, acknowledgement.

I asked her what she would have liked teachers to have done to help her.

I would perhaps have liked someone to say, look, we know you've got more ability, you're being a bit silly, what's going on? But no one ever did.

I asked what she would have liked them to say and do about her fear of exams.

I'd have liked just to be—perhaps reassured, more than anything. Told that you can only do as well as you can. A quiet chat would have been nice.

Instead of which she was given the weary old formulae: not working hard enough; work harder.

Simplicity

Perhaps there isn't time for much complexity. With the syllabus not yet completed, and the date of the exam getting closer, teachers' anxiety expresses itself in great impatience. In their impatience, they call on the soiled old stock of pedagogic simplicities. She who does not come up to scratch is lazy. She must work harder. An explanation is produced as if on the basis of thorough knowledge of the pupil, derived from close relationship. Her ineffectual work is attributed to a trait of her character: she is *lazy*. The answer? Listen to her superiors, and become *not lazy*.

The implication is that motivation can be switched on and off at will. Jane, well-defended, quiet, pleasant, is seen as sensible. Her demeanour was perhaps bound to lead to that tag. Being so sensible, how can she not have the sense to activate herself and get to work?

. . . she does not extend that good sense sufficiently to her work.

I see a robot-like creature with a reservoir of good sense stored in a component of her mind, like a battery. By flicking a switch, she has the power to enhance her academic work.

Her teacher said: 'We expect some improvement.' Not having time to apply her sensitivity, shrewdness, and great intelligence to Jane's complexity, she cannot see the irony of the way she exhorts Jane to extend her good sense. (It so happens that I know Jane's English teacher, the form teacher who made this comment, and I have respect for her.) Her remarks, and those of Jane's other teachers at this time, all imply that if she does not suddenly become sensible, she will fail her imminent exams. But *any* mention of exams produces in Jane a reaction of fear, so that she has to dig deeper; bury, deny, smile. Mention of exams, instead of doing what was intended, guaranteed that she would not do enough work.

Thus can simplification lead to fatuous mismanagement.

That's the trouble with the reports: the personality is a complicated thing, and they're saying, no, it isn't, you're *like that*.

I find that a suggestive remark. I take it to mean that Jane now feels that at school she was seen as demeaningly straightforward; that what she knows as the complexity of her mind and personality was somehow missed by her teachers, and that they did not try to fathom her.

This simplification had guaranteed that she was by her O level year almost incapable of working any harder. Just as Roger was entrenched behind his meagre theory of his ability, and not to be winkled out by his

teachers' irritable and erratic attention, so Jane had come to deny the importance of what was being offered her, out of a long-established fear; and built the theory that she wasn't very able and would never pass exams. But without exploring her beliefs, her theories, there was no chance of her teachers reversing or challenging them.

Much of what teachers say to their recalcitrant pupils is like a Frenchman giving orders to a Russian in French, thinking him stupid when he doesn't carry them out and expressing disappointment at his failure to do so.

What if Jane had been more demanding?

What difference would it have made if Jane had been more demanding? Imagine that she is a question-asker, a bright and eager member of classes; but that, immured behind her fear of exams and her contention that they don't really matter, she still doesn't work very much. Let's say that she has become, on the whole, bored and disenchanted, like Paul; but that she cannot help joining in and asking questions: taking an active part in every discussion.

Let's say that with one teacher in particular, her participation some-times makes her genuinely excited, which leads to an occasional, uncharacteristic, very successful piece of written work. And then she flunks an exam. But the teacher concerned *knows* how lively her mind is from her talkative presence in class; and she *knows* how good some of her work can be. She is, as a result, armed to fight that exam failure.

Suppose that this teacher is Jane's biology teacher, a young enthusiast. Imagine that their discussions acquire the extra dimension—the subtle extra—of affection; that she becomes interested in Jane as a person; that she acknowledges Jane in her enigmatic individuality, and is determined not to accept her exam failure. She knows that for Jane's true fulfilment she must get a handful of credentials so that she can go on to have some higher education.

What will she do? *She will talk to Jane*. She will probably talk to other teachers as well; and, who knows, she may discover that the complicated girl has done the same thing in other subjects, and that even teachers who do not like her so much are intrigued to know what made her flunk their exams too. Many a 'quiet chat' may well result, and the sort of ingenious strategy to 'rescue' a pupil that teachers are good at contriving when their interest and concern are engaged.

Soon she might have had a unanimous phalanx of teachers ranged

against her, determined to challenge and reverse her belittling theories of her worth, and to offer her ways of overcoming her fear of exams.

But nobody knew Jane that well; and there were other more pressing problems to deal with. She did not do well in her exams: passed two O levels and a few CSEs. She stayed on in the sixth form to try for a few more O levels; but nothing had changed, and a report after her first term mentions her 'casual attitude'—a new phrase to add to the running commentary.

Half-way through the year, she found herself her clerical job, and left school.

I went to see the head, told her I was leaving, she gave me a form, that was it.

How did her other teachers react, I asked.

I don't think there was any reaction. I think I just quietly walked out of school on Friday.

I think that Jane, of all the other witnesses I have called, was most like Anne, in that a sort of fear governed her avoidance of school's demands. Like all uncorroborated autobiographical evidence, her story is open to the charge that it is biased by a wish in hindsight to justify failure, or comparative failure. I have to be the interpreter of the evidence; and I have decided to trust my insight into her nature, and to accept what she says about her terror of exams.

I do not find it hard to believe. I have worked with adolescent girls at the Ashby Unit, whose mental health has been subverted by their fear of exams. I recall working, painstakingly and unsuccessfully day after day, to persuade an anorexic girl that working *less* would free her mind for greater competence. She had reached a stage at which too much work— so afraid she was of failing her exams if she did not work so hard—was gradually leading to mental paralysis. I remember working with another girl whose breakdown had been directly precipitated by overworking for her mock exams.

Their cases were extreme; Jane's represents, perhaps, an enormous number of pupils who, rather than being destroyed by their fear, neutralize it by demoting the importance of its cause; by producing an efficient neurotic defence.

For Jane is a complicated mixture: a compound of great strength and great anxiety; of nervousness and stubbornness. Stubbornly she held to her defence and did less and less work; neurotically the fear of exams fixed that defence. Stubbornly, she presented a face of quiet contentment

to her teachers; neurotically—I suspect—she told herself she was pretty mediocre anyway, so what was the point of working?

All that busy interior life never seen, perhaps never suspected by her teachers. A story never told; a girl generalized, relegated, abandoned to Nomansland. Jane feels that Nomansland was heavily populated:

that was most of my friends really—the majority of the class in my view. You get about three or four troublemakers, then you get maybe—I don't know—five or six really intelligent ones [cf. Roger] who are going to be pushed—

It is interesting that it seems to be something she took for granted that these pupils would earn plenty of attention and interest—which 'pushing' implies.

—and then I think that the majority of the class are just there and they're taught, and they're good *and* they're quiet—

Note the emphasis on 'taught', as if what was being described was some sort of automatous assembly.

—which is the way classes are. And, I mean, the reports that were churned out at the end of the year all read the same for all of us. 'Seems to be of average intelligence . . . could try harder . . . could do better if she worked harder . . .'

It is the word 'seems' that needs to be emphasized in this last telling sequence. This is the word that mediates so many of teachers' decisions about inhabitants of Nomansland. Teachers look inattentively at their biddable, uninteresting pupils. They come to decisions about those pupils which they express by the use of this most telling word: these pupils *seem* to have such and such a nature; *seem* to possess such and such an ability.

'Seem' suggests a difference between appearance and reality. But for those in Nomansland, semblance is accepted as sufficient evidence for decision and judgement; or misjudgement.

Jane seemed a sensible, pleasant girl. As she was that sort of person, her teachers decided that her lack of industry must be either from some appropriately 'sensible' decision, or from laziness. Her semblance did not allow for more complex reasons for her not working. 'Laziness' was compatible with her being pleasant and sensible, but fear or a sense of failure were not—so such feelings were not suspected. Her teachers, too, could accept her departure with equanimity, having probably decided that she had come to a 'sensible' decision about her life: 'I am not going to be an academic sort of person, but a sensible-clerk-person.'

After five years of the life she so sensibly and disastrously chose, Jane at work is bored, frustrated and intellectually starved. But she has also gained confidence; and she has at last decided to leave her job, look for part-time work, and return to education.

Those who seek refuge in Nomansland shut its doors discreetly and inaudibly behind them. I suggest that all too few manage in later life to bang them open again. Jane is brave and strong; many are not.

Her story, then, is of complexity simplified; of ambiguity unseen. Her predicament was of great ambiguity. It was as if her strength and her weakness were in equipoise: her strength the determination not to show fear or admit to feelings of failure; her weakness the fear itself—of examinations and failure. I guess that in her last years at school, smiling and pleasant and sensible, she was in a state of great confusion; she did not know whether she was clever or not, lazy or not, pleasant or not. To resolve her ambiguity—to force clarity—she decided that she wasn't very intelligent, that she wasn't the sort of person to be an academic success. She adopted an all too meagre theory of her ability and worth.

Her strength was great and allowed her to produce a strong and effective denial of her difficulties. But her difficulties were great too: her fear of exams was powerful. Ambiguity unseen: it was as if her strength and her fear neutralized each other, cancelled each other out. The result: the semblance of a pleasant, settled nature; of someone who had come, lazily but how pleasantly, to a decision about herself that would be valid for the rest of her life.

It is perhaps true of Nomansland that its members' demeanour is the calm, the disguised tension of ambiguity. Jane's stalemate is over: her fears are no longer powerful enough to contain her strength. She has become more volatile, less stable. Her loss of stability has been salvation: stability, which, in her last years at school, disguised ambiguity and confusion which no teachers suspected.

Ambiguity

Adolescence is surely the time of life when we are most likely to feel ambiguity in our ideas of ourselves and the world; to endure complexity which we deepen by our own confused reactions to it.

I do not believe in the Adolescent Identity Crisis, which seems to me a dubiously romantic idea—of a time of storm and stress out of which the man or woman emerges. But I do believe that the greater the degree of complexity an adolescent feels in her life, and the keener the ambiguity of her predicament—the more complicated her experiments will become. It also seems to me probable that *all* adolescents enter a phase of *some* complexity and ambiguity.

That phase is most likely to occur between the ages of 14 and 16: just when most is expected of pupils in school; when the people whose stories I have told were relegated to Nomansland—shelved and simplified; when what they needed from adults was subtlety, imagination, and acknowledgement of their individuality—not simplicity and generalization.

Disappearance in Nomansland

David, Anne, Paul, Roger, Jane—all spent most of their schooling in Nomansland. They spent thousands of hours on the periphery: uninvolved, disenchanted. They were quiet. They neither asked nor answered questions. They knew little intellectual excitement; neither did they know any of their teachers—with a very few exceptions—or attract their teachers' interest and concern.

All were passing through a time of life in which a person's main task is to find out what sort of adult he or she is going to become. By the time they arrived in secondary school, all had ideas of themselves that they were in the process of testing. Some of these ideas were of their intellectual capacity and their academic potential. David, Anne, and Paul thought little of their abilities when they were in secondary school. Luckily, after they left school, their ideas of their abilities were elevated. But first, David had to go through a prolonged and painful breakdown; and Anne had to wait nearly twenty years before she found herself in the hands of skilful, tactful, sensitive teachers. Paul did not have to wait so long; but he too had to depend on luck to meet teachers at his FE college who showed interest in him and acknowledged him.

But what of Roger, whom I judge to be highly intelligent? What of Alasdair and John, whom I relegated so successfully? What of Jane, whose teachers gave her so little of their attention, irritably condemning her to CSE in several subjects, allowing the evidence of her unfulfilled ability to gather dust on their shelves until it was eventually forgotten, and they began to assume she was what she *seemed* to be: a nice girl, but not particularly bright?

She now has the opportunity to recover her chances. But she will need persistence and luck to overcome the difficulties that all face who make a second attempt to educate themselves. I think she will succeed. But for Roger and many like him, education is probably over, his chance of intellectual fulfilment gone for good.

All whose stories I have told were largely unknown by their teachers. And yet all were confidently judged, and blithely abandoned to those judgements. David was most grievously misapprehended; but the others, too, were over-simplified, and assumed to *be* what they *seemed*.

Their teachers neither knew nor acknowledged them. Their complexity—often cleverly concealed—was ignored, not investigated. All of them were enigmatic; but almost no teachers tried to solve them. The teachers were not intrigued by their silence, passivity, restraint; the teachers did not refuse to be put off by their unresponsiveness, and lavish time and attention and love on them until they finally did respond. If a relationship, miraculously, did develop with a teacher, it was at the pupil's initiative, and not the teacher's; and we can assume that all the teachers—including myself—whose stories I have told, were thankful that some of their pupils, at least, could be left to 'get on with it'.

For all of them worked. Even Roger, deaf to exhortation to produce more, produced some work. All were on the whole quiet and passive; and all will have been seen to a great extent as allies in the class war. Even after I had relegated Alasdair, I was always pleased to see him in my room, because I knew he would give me no trouble. Jane, though relegated in many of her subjects to CSE, though told in many of her reports that she must work harder—was told again and again in those same reports that she was 'pleasant'. She pleased her teachers because she gave them no trouble, and got on with her work quietly.

Teachers cannot know all their pupils, nor be aware of their complexity. The passive and quiet ones are allies, because they release teachers to enjoy the company of the members of their 'families', and to get to know them in their uniqueness; and they give teachers greater freedom to control the manipulations and machinations of their 'enemies'.

That is what David's teacher meant when he told us at the Ashby Unit that David was a 'model pupil'. The fact that such a comment can be made about a pupil who was failing so grievously is a measure of the severity of the problem I am trying to illuminate: the problem of disappearance in Nomansland.

It is also a measure of teachers' helplessness to treat all their pupils wisely, scrupulously, and with sensitivity and imagination. Teachers teach crowds. One adult with a crowd of pupils is not free to work intelligently and successfully with all her pupils.

I now want to present an account of my experience of observing one particular crowd.

PART TWO

Watching a class at work. What I learnt.
What I saw. What it felt like.

CHAPTER SIX

Observing a crowd in a middle school

CLASS 4B was the crowd I chose to observe. Middle schools cater for children from 9 to 13, and often operate like primary schools: the class stays together, and teachers come to it, rather than the other way round. So I was able to find a senior class to follow from lesson to lesson. I chose 13-year-olds, because they were embarking on adolescence, and because had it not been for the middle school system they would have spent two years in secondary school already.

The school was small by secondary standards: some 400 strong. Its atmosphere was warm and friendly: walls were covered with paintings; children tended to smile at me; teachers were hospitable, and the head and his deputy were very welcoming and helpful. I am very grateful to them, and to all their colleagues who let me sit in their classes and watch.

I wanted to do just that: to watch; to see what sort of children seemed prominent, what sort less so; to see how teachers approached their pupils, and how pupils avoided and approached their teachers.

Back in the classroom

First, a disclaimer. I have much to say of a critical nature, but none of it is directed at that particular school and those particular teachers—rather at the lethargic conventions that dominate life in schools. I saw what it is difficult not to call bad teaching; but to call it that is to comment not so much on the individual teachers themselves, but on what frustrates and constrains them.

Depressing was a feeling I quickly developed of vicarious boredom. Progressing from lesson to lesson with the same class, I was to some extent infected by what they were feeling. And dreary it often was. By the end of the day, I had like them become at war with a sort of numbness, an intellectual drowsiness, the result of having been told too much for too long, without being asked to tell anything myself.

Like them, too, at the end of a lesson I felt release, an uplift, an almost manic jump of spirits. The teachers were most of them good at what they were doing: good at informing and explaining, and formidably good at controlling and demanding. During lessons the chances of release were few; so after they were over, the sense of escape was very great.

I endured lessons when a teacher spoke for nearly the whole of the thirty-five minutes allotted, and not one child uttered once. I endured others when what the teacher was saying was almost inaudible—but the class was silent. I endured lessons when the teacher seemed to be haranguing the class for reasons which were far from clear—in a style of oppressive disparagement and exhortation, the effect of which was mysteriously depressing—until I realized that it had awakened my own memories of pessimistic pedagogy: that style of teaching that always expects the worst, and always, always finds it. I endured, too, extremely well-taught lessons, the intellectual content of which was pitifully demeaning.

I sympathized with the ingenious tactics pupils seemed to have devised to help them pass the dreary hours; their careful vigilance while doing something illegitimate; their ability to amuse themselves trivially for long stretches of time. I admired, for instance, the persistent craftiness of one boy—Ginger, to whom I shall return later—who made almost no contact with his teachers, and who did, as far as I could see, a well-judged modicum of work; but who, as soon as he knew he was safe from attention, would hold long, lively conversations with a neighbour, which would have been impossible to overhear from even six inches away. His otherwise drowsy, unenlivened features would light up and become attractive and funny, and his gestures would become as fluent and full of meaning as a mime's.

I endure the drudging sluggishness of school time—time unlike all other time, unless you are lucky enough to be teaching rather than being taught. I was busy; but I felt the slowness of its passing. It was like watching a ponderous, silted river.

However, I also witnessed some very skilful teaching, when many pupils were engaged in what they were doing. And I saw moments of tact and subtlety; when teachers dealt with difficulty and dissent without being censorious or oppressive. *And all the time*—with very few exceptions—I was in the presence of teachers of whose concern for their charges there was not the slightest doubt; and whose kindness was impressive. The word is too bland: tenderness would be a better word: they could show a solicitous tenderness that was sometimes moving to witness.

I recall the maths teacher approaching a child whose unhappiness that day was palpable. The quality of his presence, and the degree—not too intrusive, not too public—of his warmth and reassurance, were so well judged, so convincing. He talked about her work, but their conversation was about far more.

I felt keenly the gulf between what these impressive people could and should be; and what they seemed in school to have become. For they always seemed on the run; they always seemed never quite *there*, never focused precisely on what they were doing. And their rituals—their insistence on the date in the top right corner of the page; their going steadily through the vocabulary; their, 'I'll go through it once again on the board and then you try it,'—all had a somnambulist quality.

They carried their kindness with them like an atmosphere; they had become skilled tacticians of the avoidance of confrontation; but their intellects seemed asleep.

I felt, too, all the time, a nagging certainty that the style of learning of which I was a witness was ineffectual and mistaken. I shall turn to that style of learning in Chapter Eight.

What I sat out to do was to record, by manic writing down of everything I saw, every contact made between a teacher and a pupil. I could not hope to catch every single contact. But I did aim to do a gross arithmetic of the relations between teachers and pupils that I saw being enacted before me. I devised a code, and a way of writing briefly and quickly a description of what I saw. And I included all sorts of contact, from a question asked, to a reprimand given; from a meaningful shake of the head, to a shared laugh without words.

There were moments when so much contact was being made so fast—for instance, during a French lesson, when questions were being asked about a text the class had read, and hands were shooting up to answer them—that I must have missed some contacts made. But there were more frequent phases of lessons when contact was less often, and much more easily recordable. Moreover, the phases of most rapid contact tended to be with the same pupils, again and again. In French, to take the best example, the teacher waited for hands to go up before asking her quick-fire questions; and the same hands tended to go up on each occasion. And interestingly, when she chose people to read, or to stumble through what they had written out loud, she chose the same people, the question-answerers. So I am pretty sure that I missed contacts only with those pupils whom teachers tended to contact most frequently, rather than with the elusive and least often contacted.

Nomansland was visibly there to be watched—where skulked some crafty boys, and douce and biddable girls. Passivity was there, as a style, a demeanour, a ritualized way of being. Anonymity was there; or not there. Without thinking it out very clearly, I decided not to ask teachers for the names of the pupils I was watching, so that I could become acquainted with names naturally, according to the frequency of their use. I disobeyed my own rule stupidly with one girl, Mona, who intrigued me so much from the start that I asked a teacher for her name, before I could stop myself. But otherwise I knew no names until I heard them used.

One girl's name I still did not know after two weeks and over seventy lessons. Several girls' names I did not know until well on in the second week. Only one boy's name escaped me till then; and I knew his by the first day of the second week.

The disparity between the most and the least contacted was startling—amazing. A boy, Darren, scored 123 contacts. A girl, Jenny, scored only 7. Boys on the whole made more contact with their teachers than girls. There were twelve boys in the class and they achieved in total 626 contacts. There were more girls in the class—sixteen—but they made only 489 contacts.

It was also interesting that those towards the top of the list of contacts—the active, the attractive—tended to volunteer, to initiate contact; but those from the middle of the list downwards were, on the whole, more contacted than contacting.

Those at the bottom of the list were barely contacted at all, nor did they make contact. They spoke not, neither did they attract. The last eight on the list—ranging from 16 contacts to 7—were all girls.

The literature on the predicament of girls in schools is impressive. I have no doubt that decorum and passivity are subtly purveyed in schools as the 'proper demeanour for women'. I shall discuss this issue in the next chapter.

I saw, in the most passive and least contacted, girls who smiled and were helpful; who were reticent and comely; whose shyness—bringing a slight blush to their cheeks when approach was made—was graceful and insidiously pleasing to watch. I could recall my own vague pleasure in the presence of such girls when I was a teacher: girls who dressed neatly and wrote nicely; who made my feeble jokes welcome; who never gave trouble; who belched not, neither did they fart.

There has been interesting research recently that suggests that in mixed schools, girls are excluded from subjects like physics and chemistry, but that they are likely to choose biology and arts subjects. To my mind, even more interesting has been research that has concerned what takes place between teachers and pupils in class.

A fascinating small study by Michelle Stanworth of a mixed class at a college of further education, gives a picture of male assertiveness, competitiveness, willingness to hold the floor and argue a point—and of female reticence and avoidance of the limelight. She also suggests that teachers—men and women—are magnetized by the articulate, forceful boys to seek them out in preference to the girls, in discussion and debate.

I certainly saw boys getting a great deal of attention. The two who made most contacts were in every way attractive. They were good-looking, articulate, naughty in an agreeable way, willing to make fools of themselves, willing to help, willing to speak even if they had nothing of great relevance to say.

There is a sequence in a French lesson which is relevant. The French teacher had a persuasive, pleasant, warm manner. She smiled. She encouraged. She praised a good quick answer. She seemed to have the knack of making her pupils relax enough to risk saying something in French. She herself seemed relaxed, and to be enjoying what she was doing.

But admirable though she was in all these ways, she was unusually partial in her choice of participants. Teaching a language depends on participation: on pupils speaking, asking, risking. If she chose a pupil to speak, she chose either the always willing—like Darren or Nevin, the two 'top' contacters, neither of whom seemed especially gifted at French, but both of whom were happiest in the limelight; or she chose those who did seem gifted at French. But even these pupils—and one girl, Marilyn, in particular—she 'used' less than the two boys.

More often than not, if she were seeking answers to her questions, or the meaning of words in a text, the teacher would ask: 'Et Monsieur Dupont, qu'est-ce qu'il faisait hier, qu'est-ce qu'il faisait?' and wait for hands to go up. She would then, with unerring regularity, choose the owner of the most vociferous hand, or the hands of those she knew would give an accurate answer. Often, in the competition to be chosen, the two boys would win, and give inaccurate answers.

My notes do not tell me exactly how one particular lesson began. But soon afterwards a vocabulary test had to be done. By that time, Darren had already spoken twice, in a loud voice. The lesson began at 1.07 p.m., and the test began at 1.09 p.m. Twice then, in two minutes, Darren had frolicked in the limelight.

He had been the first of the pupils to speak to me uninvited. My profile—sitting at the back of the room with my clipboard and my carefully neutral expression—was as low as I could make it. But to Darren I was another, probably sympathetic, person to engage in conversation. 'How are you, all right?' he asked. Thereafter he would always acknowledge me in some way.

He was slightly overweight; he liked to get out of his seat and walk about, if possible—usually finding a legitimate reason to do so. He smiled, joked, laughed. He would always put his hand up and volunteer an answer to a question, even if he had not heard the question properly. His demeanour was in every way the opposite of the disengagement and passivity of Nomansland.

It became obvious that he irritated his teachers. His French teacher, the second time he spoke, had to shut him up: he was not speaking to her but to someone at the other side of the room. But she and his other teachers liked him too; and they depended on him. It was obvious that his French teacher—as I did—put a very high value on liveliness. She needed lively pupils to generate the sort of atmosphere she liked. With Darren, in whom was no malice, her irritation was less important than her appreciation.

The test finished. Then more vocabulary was tested—out loud. The class, all twenty-eight of them, had read a page of 'the book' for homework and had been asked to learn the new words.

I shall quote from my notes:

QUESTION AND ANSWER—teacher asking for volunteers.
Darren answers
Terry
Malcolm
Darren shouts out
Darren again—tremendous enthusiasm at having got a right answer.

This sequence of male participation is followed by:
1.17 p.m. Two girls in front of me still haven't said a word.

What a contrast these two girls were to Darren in all the French lessons, and in all lessons. The code for one of them was 'TH' until well into the second week: TH standing for 'tailhead', to illustrate the minuscule pigtail she wore as a relish to her short haircut. Not once in the French lessons did she contact or was she contacted.

My next entry says that Darren is waving his arm madly to answer the next question. He answers it, again with pleasure at getting it right.

Then the teacher asks to see the exercise books of those who have queries about the written part of the homework—questions to answer about the dread Duponts. Who are at the head of the line waving their books? Darren and Nevin. They and three other pupils stand at the teacher's desk. 'Très bien', I hear her say, in her warm friendly voice.

The two girls in front of me, heads well down, murmur discreetly to each other. Then the next stage of the lesson begins. The text is to be read aloud: another thrilling day in the lives of the Duponts. The text requires two readers. Darren and Nevin are both chosen.

The prominent and the ignored

It seemed to me that what had happened was that Darren, from the beginning of the lesson, had made sure that his teacher knew he was there. At first she has to admonish him—lightly—for being too noisy. But twice he answers her questions correctly, and rewards her with his delight at his success. So that when she roams the room looking for readers, his face, name, presence are pleasurably clear in her mind, and it is inevitable that she chooses him.

In all, the teacher contacted ten pupils in this lesson, out of twenty-eight. She sought out those who attracted and rewarded her, and avoided the rest. She also sought out those who, to be controlled, need a large share of the limelight. Darren is attractive; but she and his other teachers also know that if they do not give him plenty of attention, he will create his own limelight on another part of the stage.

The corollary of this suggests why the passive girls are so pleasant to teach. I have made the point already: they please because they present no problem, but *the pleasure they provide is limited*. They are not attractive enough to be rewarding; and it is as if they are trapped by the mild pleasure they provide, which confirms their timidity and the ideas they have already learnt about how to behave.

But some of the girls escaped relegation to demure complaisance; and men teachers, especially, seemed to like them.

Liz

Liz was physically more grown up than the other girls. Science was her great interest. She was apparently able to hold her own in lessons against boys who tried to tease her; she was often quiet, but also usually prepared to volunteer an answer to a teacher's question.

But in science, she exercised a curious dominance of proceedings. The teacher—a large agreeable man, with a marked ability to make what he was teaching sound interesting—tended always to ask Liz if he needed an answer to a closed question that would help to put others on the right track. (By 'closed', I mean a question with only one right answer. Research suggests that the great majority of teachers' questions are of this sort.)

The following figures suggest Liz's dominance.

Lesson 1 she scored 6 of the 38 contacts made $c.\ \frac{1}{6}$ of all

2	7	27	$c.\ \frac{1}{4}$
3	5	54	$c.\ \frac{1}{10}$
4	4	57	$c.\ \frac{1}{14}$

There were 28 pupils in the class, so in each of these lessons she scored more than her 'fair share' of contacts.

Interestingly, in all these lessons the teacher spent a significant amount of time talking to Liz in private: five minutes in Lesson 2 (a short one of thirty minutes). And in the lesson in which her number of contacts was least, she spent seven minutes (out of an hour) at the teacher's table on one occasion, and he spent three at her desk on another: making ten minutes in all, which is a very large proportion of his time to devote to one pupil.

I can clearly recall the quality of their exchanges; and my notes corroborate my memory. They spoke to each other as father and daughter. The teacher obviously loved having a pupil whose interest in his subject was so keen; and he was prepared to lavish as much time and attention on her as he could. They would laugh. He would tease her with difficult questions, and then praise her when she made an intelligent stab at an answer. She would smile in a way that made her affection obvious. When they were together, the rest of the class were forgotten. Because this teacher had a relaxed and highly effective control of his pupils, this did not create problems—though it did allow a certain amount of quiet disaffection to brew. And it seemed always to take a long time for the teacher to re-enter the public world of his class and realize that order needed to be re-established. He was usually equable and pleasant in manner; but when his private pleasure had thus to end, his irritation was obvious.

It was as if I were looking at myself as I pored over Robert's work, Mairhi's work, Shona's work. What I was witnessing was a teacher and a pupil acknowledging each other.

Meanwhile, Sophie, Nilly and Jennifer—10, 9, and 7 contacts in over seventy lessons in two weeks—plodded solemnly through their work, unacknowledged and largely unseen.

Liz was not reticent or discreet. If she wanted help, she would ask for it with a firmly raised hand. If she were annoyed by a boy, she would bark at him to shut up.

Frances

So would Frances. On page 28 of my 145 pages of notes, I read:

First disciplinary action against a girl: Frances exiled.

This took place in maths. She was sent out of the room briefly for persistent talking. But like all her teachers, her maths teacher liked Frances very much. Apart from Darren and Nevin, she seemed to me to have the most revealed personality in the class. She showed herself, all the time, in a way quite uninhibited by the presence of so many others. If she was bored, she would show it, rather than pretend in a seemly and decorous way to be quite contented. If she was angry, she would show it—and was often to be heard telling boys to shut up. If a more seemly neighbour wanted to ask a question but didn't have the courage, Frances, irritated, would speak up for her. She was very pretty; and dressed in ways that suggested affluent and doting parents.

Frances seemed to magnetize teachers. A geography lesson is illustrative. The class were in groups, sitting around tables doing their 'projects': each pupil had chosen a European country, and was writing about it, using reference books to do so. The atmosphere was relaxed and industrious. Pupils were free to talk. Frances, working hard, talked hard, too. The teacher, a youngish man with a relaxed and friendly manner similar to the science teacher's, went five times to Frances's table during the hour's lesson. On each occasion he joined in the conversation by responding to something Frances said with a joke, a witty capping comment. He might smile gently with the quiet girls; but he laughed with Frances.

Twice his visits to her table were subtly controlling. Her voice was suddenly to be heard very clearly above the rest; so the teacher went to talk to her, both to enjoy her liveliness, and also to sanction it and so neutralize its potential for disorder.

Teachers are skilled at this technique: I was too. There is nothing, for instance, more potentially hazardous to peace and work than a good loud fart. A fart is difficult to deal with. To over-react is to set up a temptation to every self-respecting sphincter in the room; but to under-react would be a dangerous sign of weakness. I developed a tactic for farters, for which I called on my seedy acting talents. I would walk slowly to a window, with an expression on my face of exaggerated and, I hoped, comical boredom. At the same time, I would mutter under my breath about toilet training and wind-control, speaking more loudly out of the window to no one, when I had opened it. By this time, everyone would be tittering civilly, and any danger would be over. I would have annexed the original fart-hilarity and made it legitimate; made it serve my purposes.

Thus to receive a fart is a subtle form of flattery of the farter. You, I implied, are powerful and important enough to lead these others astray with your breach of wind and peace. I will defeat you by being mildly amused; but I know that my amusement too is flattering.

Frances was visibly earning this sort of affirmation. Each time the teacher visited her table to talk to her, or to turn her talking to good purpose—partly controlling her, partly using his pleasant reception of her hilarity to perpetuate the relaxed atmosphere in the class, an atmosphere evidently conducive to good work—she proved herself the most important person in the room.

One of the quiet girls came to her table once to ask her advice, as if paying court. But Frances could be an irritable queen. 'Well, use coloured pencils then!', I heard her say.

To ask the question, 'What did she gain from her prominence?' is another way of asking what the quiet, the 'no-women', lost. I do have something to say, building on the stories I have already told, about the intellectual benefit of talk and participation. But I want now to consider simpler benefit and loss.

The benefit and loss of participation

Frances, like Liz, was a frequent visitor to teachers' tables, where long dialogues would take place. On such occasions, the degree to which she was acknowledged was clear. And the sort of exchanges that took place in the geography lesson told her that she, a woman, was right to speak loudly, assert herself, be honest in her demands, seek out others' attention and enjoy it.

Confirmed were her behaviour and an idea of her own importance and validity likely to stand her in good stead in later life. Unless her confidence was to go into serious recession, it was hard to imagine her browbeaten, put down, neglected.

Just before the bell rang for the end of the lesson, the teacher asked who liked playing tennis. Tailhead liked playing tennis, but she didn't want to speak. She was sitting near Frances, and Frances knew she liked tennis.

'Go on,' she said, 'tell him.' Tailhead blushed, but wouldn't speak. She hung her head. Irritated, Frances spoke for her.

'Sir, Fiona's really good at tennis, she likes it—'

This lesson took place towards the end of my second week; and that was how I first heard Fiona's name: used, in irritation, by someone speaking for her.

'Right,' said the teacher, 'Fiona likes tennis, okay—' and went on with his enquiry.

One of her teachers described Fiona to me as 'a nice shy little thing', after my two weeks were over. By being accepted as such, it is likely that a disbelief in her own importance—a theory of her *unimportance*—was being confirmed. Not to speak out, to let others speak for you, is abdication of your rightful place as just as worthy of being heard as anyone else, whatever your ability.

It would be inappropriate to load her teacher's decision to accept Frances as Fiona's spokeswoman with too much importance; but there is no doubt that it must, in however small a way, have confirmed Fiona's reticence and deference. All he said was, 'Right, Fiona', ticking off a name given by someone else as if Fiona was not in the room. He did not ask Fiona to tell him anything about her liking for tennis. Nor did he take and use an opportunity to coax her out of hiding, to feel the limelight on her face.

Consider an alternative reaction:

'Sir, sir, Fiona's good at tennis—'

'Thank you Frances, but I'm sure Fiona can speak for herself.'

Fiona now blushes, showing signs of embarrassment. There are twenty-seven other people in the room, apart from the teacher. But he knows that, daunting though the crowd may be, Fiona, like anyone else, can learn to be unafraid—if she gets enough practice and has her efforts acknowledged. He may also be wise enough to guess that her pretty-blush tactic is a learnt evasion rather than expression of an established personality trait.

Still Fiona doesn't speak. The pause lengthens. The teacher is tempted to abandon her; but he persists. Her blush deepens. He begins to feel cruel in his persistence. But he doesn't give up.

'Do you like tennis?'

'Yes.'

'Are you good at it?'

'Yes, she's very good at it,' says Frances.

'Go on, say you're good at it, there's nothing wrong with being honest.'

'I'm good at tennis,' says Fiona, all in a rush, before she knows what she's doing.

Suppose that all her other teachers are united in their sly determination to winkle Fiona out of Nomansland; that in every lesson she attends she will be held kindly in the limelight until she seeks it voluntarily. It would not take long for her to cease to need a spokeswoman.

Jane has told me that she wished someone had taught her how to ask a question. What she meant was that she regretted that no one had tried to help her to learn to cope with the embarrassment of sudden prominence, and to encourage her to believe that anything she asked would be worth asking. Many of the 'meagre hypotheses' tested and established in adolescence are based on phantasy. The most common phantasy, on which the reticent in classes build their hypotheses of unimportance, is that if they speak they will be laughed at.

To accept their reticence may be to accept their self-contempt.

Human sacrifice

Now I want to introduce you to the drama teacher, Mrs Phillips. She is a bit of a tartar. She is very good at explaining things clearly. She uses a blackboard to great effect; and her discipline is faultless. She has only to raise her voice, and all are quiet and attentive. Drama is one of her subjects. Her main one is maths; and I also watch her teaching health.

She, more than any of the other teachers, seems always to be else-where, to have become distracted. Long spells of her health lessons are harangues. The class sit them out like bad weather, hearing about the dangers of not washing their hands. But she is always impressive: her firmness, her fairness, her clarity, her well-turned sentences. And yet I feel, all the time, that her performance has become private. I sense her silent acclamation of a particular word or phrase; and her flights on health seem to be addressed not to the audience in the room with her, but to some private interior panel of pedagogues: Fabian in politics, and concerned with the inculcation of a sanitary outlook.

I like Mrs Phillips very much. Join me in one of her drama lessons.

This takes place in the school hall with the curtains drawn. A small battery of lights on stands are there to be used for atmospheric effect.

When I go in, the class are already spread loosely all over the room. Mrs Phillips is putting a record on a large old-fashioned gramophone: Mahler, very loud. It seems to have no effect on the children. Because the music is so loud, Mrs Phillips has to shout at them to sit down; which they do, cross-legged, on the floor. She walks slowly into the throng, and grabs a large boy by the arm, leading him back towards the gramophone.

'You don't like drama much, you can operate it.' she says, handing the boy a spotlight on a stand, and pointing to the dimmer board beside him.

I notice that the girls have sat in one group, the boys in another. My notes tell me that the boys are 'restless', the girls 'more contemplative'.

They all sit, taking the music as if it were another of Mrs Phillips's harangues. The music ends. The boys are told to erect an altar out of bits of dais. When this has been done, the first dramatic instruction ensues:

'Relax. You are an ancient Celtic tribe, waiting for the full moon.'

There follows a short discussion of some of the things the tribe has been doing while it waits. Obviously much of the scene has been organized in previous lessons. First they have to go to sleep and wake up. The girls do this slowly and elegantly, the boys very quickly; and soon some of the boys are on their feet. Nevin is instantly in the spotlight—the moon, now risen—shading his eyes and looking around. Some are breaking firewood; others are skinning a rabbit. I hear them discussing this, and the gruesome mime becomes intelligible.

The girls do less, and less intelligibly. They wander, and eventually sit down again.

'Face the light and do something', says Mrs Phillips.

Nevin and Darren are in the spotlight, worshipping it lackadaisically.

'You're going to be sick doing that, change your pattern of behaviour,' they are told.

But there's a general subsidence, a loss of energy; so Mrs Phillips calls them all to order for a discussion of what to do next. I find myself now admiring the way she draws suggestions out; but those who make them are those who always volunteer.

Enthusiasm returns with general agreement that a queue should form to worship the moon, two by two. As each pair approaches the altar, they are to *recognize* each other. Mrs Phillips chooses Nevin to demonstrate what she means, delivering a small Celtic bow to the boy, who returns it more expressively. Someone should be on the altar, too. Nevin and Darren are the first to climb up. Mrs Phillips shoos them away, and elects one of the tallest girls in the class as high priestess, but avoids her name (so that I still do not catch it—about half-way through my first week).

Darren and Nevin manage to be at the head of the queue. Darkness falls. Mahler returns, more quietly. The moon slowly rises.

'Darren and Nevin go forward,' Mrs Phillips hisses. Theirs are the only names mentioned.

They walk smartly forward, forgetting to recognize each other, then remembering, and performing elaborate, mocking obeisance, bowing and scraping and taking off ancient Celtic top hats. They thus set a tone of just acceptable mickey-taking for the rest of the boys.

The girls are perfunctory in their worship. My notes say:

W, TG and Liz come on and worship, en route for the shops

After they and two others have finished, they sit:

W, TG, Greenlegs, Liz and Frances [note the mixture of code for names not yet known, and names for those already familiar] are in a corner: Celts picnicking in the lunch hour.

Frances is the only girl to worship with enthusiasm. Soon a pause of general worship ensues, all clustered at the altar to do so. Spontaneously, a group decides on a human sacrifice. To my glee, they choose a girl who has interested me from the start, whose name I asked for, spoiling my tactic: Mona.

Willingly Mona lets herself be plonked on the altar, a knife is stuck into her by the priestess, and her corpse is carted off to the window. The expression on her face is of mild and civil pleasure: if they want to sacrifice me, that's fine by me.

It was a good moment to see Mona sacrificed, because I had marked her down as the most perfectly compliant, elegantly, discreetly nice of all in the class. Those girls who appear at the bottom of my list are indecipherable, so blank and unresponsive were they in all the lessons I witnessed. But Mona was different. Though passive, she seemed in some way definite, finished. Though she did not volunteer answers to questions very often, she would seek help from her teachers from time to time, by going to their tables with her book. And if a teacher asked her a question directly, using her name, she would try to answer it; though with what I felt was well-acted diffidence.

She seemed to have perfected a pleasing demeanour. She was unfailingly deferential, and well behaved. My notes are littered with:

And Mona is working, head down . . .

I contrived to see her exercise books from time to time. They were neat. Her dates and headings were underlined. She was one of the three girls who looked after the animals in science, clearing out their cages, cleaning, feeding them.

What she seemed to have achieved was a dissociation of public and private: between the requirements of school and class life, and the pleasures of being a member of a small group of friends. Her public self was complaisant, biddable, decorous; and two of her teachers told me she was 'very grown up'. Her contacts—50 of them, placing her exactly in the middle of the list—tended to be very brief, and only semi-public: made at the teacher's desk, or when the teacher was wandering around the room looking at work, or at the end of lessons.

At no time did she show signs of excitement, or any great interest or curiosity. Her demeanour was that of a good girl who likes to be busy. She always sat next to a friend, to whom she would whisper discreetly. Her private smile could be almost broad; but her public smile was sweet and nice.

Sometimes she crossed the boundary from private to public. Twice she raised her voice to tell a boy not to do something—to leave her books alone, to give back her pen; and on both occasions she put her hand up to her mouth as if to say, 'oh dear, what have I done?' At another time she belched, and went through the same pantomime of self-admonishment.

I felt as if her public self, in an equivalent way, were as automatic and dissociated as some of her teachers seemed to be as they went solemnly through their days; as if she and they, skilled somnambulists all, had met in their sleep and negotiated their agreement to pay a certain amount of attention to each other, but not too much—Mona offering neat work in exchange for the promise of infrequent visits to her desk: her teachers offering her their mild pleasure in exchange for her mild presence.

The bargain once sealed, she kept to her side of it consistently and loyally. So how could her teachers have quarrelled with her? With that mild contentment most of all? I know nothing about her ideas of herself—though I shall speculate in the next chapter; and I know nothing about her ability—except that her teachers subsequently told me she was 'average'. But her contented air might have been cover for all sorts of faulty decisions about her ability and herself.

Towards the end of the drama lesson she offered herself for sacrifice again—civilly and willingly. Frances let out a bloody yell as the knife went in; but it was impossible to imagine them changing places.

CHAPTER SEVEN

Belittled women: the feminist case

I WANT now to consider Mona and the girls in her class who made less contact with teachers than she did, including those who made almost no contact at all.

That is the most startling feature of what I saw: that some girls made almost no contact with teachers, and *most* girls seemed more disengaged and less involved in what was going on than *most* of the boys. The drama lesson illustrates this last contention. Girls on the whole—Frances excepted—wandered about, sought each other's company to form quiet, vaguely contented little groups, vaguely carried out their—vague— instructions. Boys mastered their predicament: how to enjoy and make sense of a loosely structured lesson which allowed them freedom from the constraints of normal school work. They took initiatives—Darren and Nevin when they made their elaborate bows, or the little group skinning a rabbit. They joined in.

But the girls' participation was so perfunctory that it was really a disguise: ritual not actual; gesture to avert awareness of their disen- gagement. They made sense of their predicament by neutralizing it. The only two prominent girls, apart from Frances, were the high priestess— who carried out her instructions obediently and energetically enough—and her victim, whose prominence was not chosen, and who distinctly underplayed when the role was forced on her. No screams, death-rattle, or writhing from Mona. Hers was a discreet death.

The arithmetic of the girls' comparative neglect by their teachers, the negligible amount of contact made by the girls lowest on the list, and the boys' comparative monopoly of attention should, I feel, startle. The biographies I have already written here suggest that nice, pleasing, inactive girls may be concealing discontent and lack of fulfilment. But from teachers, what I saw being enacted before me was a *wholesale acceptance* of niceness, pleasantness, and passivity.

Clearly, the 'niceness' was helpful, releasing teachers to deal with their more demanding or more attractive pupils. But though teachers may have been thus responding to the constraint of class size, I believe that their acceptance of 'niceness' was also acceptance of the proper demeanour for young women.

The exceptions suggested that I was seeing enacted the belief that there will always be some 'remarkable women'; but that most will be pleasant, ordinary, content not to stand out, not to take many risks. I was seeing a mass-simplification, a sleight-of-mind by which teachers could accept the blandness and passivity of so many of their pupils as right and proper, because they were female.

I shall explore these matters by way of a speculation about Mona and others—about a composite person, Mona-Joanne-Kerry—MJK for short. MJK is a history: of the transformation of Mona, the middle school pupil contented and smiling, into Joanne at a comprehensive—a little less contented; who eventually becomes Kerry—depressed and cheated until she arrives at a college of further education.

Mona

Let us suppose that what I guess to have been Mona's negotiation of a way of being in school was prompted initially by her perception of herself as a busy girl whose sums and stories were quite good, but not very good.

Let us suppose that loving parents had brought her up strictly but kindly to be neat, tidy, and well behaved; and that their precepts about what girls should be like helped to prepare the demeanour which came to suit her so well in school.

Imagine, for instance, that she learnt early on to accept that being greedy for attention was 'bad', and that being quiet and nice were 'good'; and that her parents, in her early childhood, tended to satisfy her curiosity mildly and forgetfully, rather than with enthusiasm and delight. Imagine, too, that she learnt that the best way of pleasing adults was a kind of precocious moderation: a lack of excessive show, excessive interest, excessive demands, excessive resentments.

She will have found, soon, in school that this learned moderation was very pleasing to harassed primary school teachers with over thirty pupils in their classes. Flagrant curiosity she had already learnt to associate with greed and selfishness; so from the outset, the waving hand and shout for 'Miss!' were not for her, and she became one of the pupils on whom her teachers could depend to make steady unremarkable progress, assiduously and pleasantly.

As her school career steadily progressed, she will have seen herself more and more irretrievably as the good little worker her teachers took her to be. This self-perception must have meant that when she was given work to do, she saw the task as a chance to exercise her teacher-friendly neatness, deftness and complaisance, rather than offering the possibility of excitement or novelty. A child's or an adolescent's theories about herself determine, perhaps to a great extent, the way her mind works. Mona, seeing herself as a neat, busy, unexcitable worker, made her mind function in ways necessary to produce neat, busy, unexcitable work.

Mona's school career was a conspiracy between a restrictive idea of herself and teachers' need for quiet little workers to help create peace and order in their classrooms. And what made it easier for this bargain to be struck was that Mona's behaviour was the proper behaviour for a woman in the making.

One of a possible number of selves

Liam Hudson, in *Frames of Mind*, reports an experiment which suggests the power of self-perception to affect the way a mind works. Mona saw herself as a good little girl. In Hudson's work, two groups of boys think of themselves respectively as 'convergers' and 'divergers'; and he suggests that, just as Mona's idea of herself has its origins partly in precepts about proper femininity, the boys' self-perceptions are not explicable only in terms of individual psychology.

Briefly, convergers are analytic, pragmatic—able to clarify and narrow down issues by means of systematic dismissal of inessentials. Divergers are florid, inventive, figurative—able to widen issues to accommodate many implications by means of intuitive flights of analogy.

Hudson gave both groups a test which asked them to suggest as many ways as possible in which certain objects could be used; for instance, a milk bottle. Convergers were practical, a little dull. Divergers were amusing, sometimes lurid, always surprising.

But the next stage of the experiment is what fascinates. He asked the convergers to do the test again, imagining themselves to be a Bohemian artist, characterized for them in detail. In other words, by means of a sort of role-play, he offered them a chance to try out a quite different self-perception. The results were startling. Convergers became divergers, and the luridness and obscenity of some of their suggestions implied that their converger self-perception contained a fair degree of repression.

This is a beautiful suggestion of the power of self-perception to affect the way *minds* set to work on *tasks*. It is also very suggestive of the value of offering opportunity for release from restrictive self-perception. This, I suspect, is what—all unknowing—we did at the Ashby Unit when we asked David to think of himself as an aggressive prosecuting lawyer; by means of which ruse, dormant ability could jump awake. And Mona may have been presenting to the world only one of a number of possible selves.

The implication is startling. Teachers, by accepting the self they see, with gratitude and approval—gratitude for its helpfulness, approval of its femininity—are imprisoning others. Among them, perhaps, may be a self more authentically expressive of needs, talents and compulsions than the self being presented.

M, then, is the selection, for Woman proceeding through English education of a minimal self, and its confirmation by others.

This stage is accompanied by considerable contentment. Mona basks in the tepid warmth of adults' benign gratitude and their appreciation of her womanliness—just as Darren goes his cheery way, eased by the plenary indulgence that 'boys will be boys'.

Mona and her teachers are quite happy with the busy-little-worker self she has chosen to stitch—so nimbly and neatly—for her life.

But will her contentment last? Now consider Joanne.

Joanne

Joanne was in the fifth year at the comprehensive school where I carried out research. She seemed to her teachers to be quite happy. But I judge her contentment in school to have been at a critical stage; that it was in the process of fading. I believe that the impression she gave teachers— avoiding their attention as far as possible, getting on with her work obediently but without interest, aiming her ambitions at being an office worker, so not pushing herself too hard—was misleading.

When I interviewed her, she seemed to be rather like Roger: cautious, intelligent, watchful. I liked her. She listened to my questions and considered her answers with either shyness or assurance—it was hard to decide which. Her manner was in all ways feminine: discreet, elegant, reticent.

She sat in her armchair, legs demurely and neatly crossed at ankle, uniform of dark skirt and dark pullover in some subtle way enhanced to elegance, suggesting a carefully chosen ensemble for a day at work, not schoolgirlish at all. I realized, not long after we had begun our interview, that I was treating her and thinking of her as if she were an attractive woman of 23 or 24, and not a girl of 16. She seemed poised, complete. It was as if her air of slight shyness was itself 'grown up': a sort of decorous evasiveness, a veiling, a modest detachment.

Joanne liked typing.

I want a career as an office worker, so obviously I'm going to try to enjoy my job, and typing's a part of it. It's a lesson where I can get down to it.

This is Mona, a stage further on in her career. She has opted for being busy. She has opted for business. Note that she has to *tell* herself that typing is enjoyable. There is no spontaneous admission of pleasure. 'I'm going to try to enjoy my job, so I'm trying to enjoy typing, which is a preparation for it.' Deliberate self-management is suggested, in accord with her quiet elegance.

Note also that most of her teachers nominated her as someone who showed herself little, whom they found difficult to know. And note that her reports hum with mild appreciation, the repeated distant buzzing of the word 'please' and all its variants:

She has worked conscientiously and made pleasing progress. I hope she will develop more confidence with oral work.

says her French teacher, a year before I met her, implying that it was up to Joanne to change—to find that confidence. Interesting too is the word 'pleasing'. Her oral work is not good enough; and in fact, shortly afterwards, she gives up French altogether. And yet she has made 'pleasing progress'. I take this to mean: 'She has quietly done the written work set. She has given me no trouble, unlike some of the others.'

Joanne likes biology:

I like biology, but we never seem to do anything.

When Joanne was Mona, being busy but inactive—rather than busily creative—didn't worry her. Being busy was rewarding enough. But the scales are slowly falling from Joanne's eyes:

Half the time you don't need to ask questions anyway because we're just copying off the board.

Mona would never have added that word 'just'. When Joanne was Mona, copying was fun.

I get very bored [in biology] especially in a double lesson.

And this is a subject she says she enjoys.

Her typing teacher has accepted that she has become what she was always ordained to become. She subsumes her into a small group of girls:

All those girls have settled much more into their personalities [their personalities, held out for them like clothes] . . . they haven't got to worry about their characters now, they're more interested in their work.

What else should she have thought of Joanne, doing her good neat work?

Her English teacher—a subject she said she didn't like—is aware that a choice has been made, and an alternative abandoned. He is to some extent aware of complexity. But he is conscious, too, of the limits set on what he can do; and evidently believes that he should not try to extend them:

I've hoped that she would turn out better than she is now [as usual, this change is *up to the pupil*: teachers are helpless to help—much]. She does some very good work, but she doesn't insist on herself being very good. She might not be very good, but I've got this feeling that she might be . . .

I ask how the impression of her not being very good comes across.

Well, she just tends to do the job and behave like a bank girl, but every so often she does something better than that and she's rather surprised that you think highly of it, and pleased, and can be encouraged to branch out in that way again.

But it seems that he just has to accept his lack of time and opportunity for such encouragement:

But I'm quite happy. I've taught many students, mainly girls I think, I guess this is chiefly a thing to do with girls—who could be terrific if they wanted to, but have been quite happy to be bank girls. Nice steady job, nice steady life and who's to say there's anything wrong with that?

Nothing, perhaps—so long as she has been offered and has tried out some alternatives.

He admits, a little later, that when Joanne does a 'very good' piece of work, she treats her success as an aberration, and quickly returns to normal—to her prematurely secretarial mediocrity. And he has not made it a priority to seize these moments and use them to force her to consider another idea of herself. Being a bank girl is okay, who is to say it isn't?

Drama: another self out of hiding

In drama, another moment occurred, when an alternative perception of herself flashed out of hiding. What happened next is very illuminating. I shall quote the whole dialogue when Joanne described this experience.

Me: Are you ever envious of people who do the opposite of you—who love discussion and do a lot of noisy talking and get quite excited?

Jo: Sometimes, it depends what the subject is.

Me: Can you give me an example of when that might be?

Jo: Well, in drama I sometimes wish I could be more outspoken, I don't know why I'm not.

She also added:

> I'd just like to join in more than what I do. A lot of the time I'll sit there and listen. I'll sit and listen and sometimes I'll talk, but I like to listen rather than put my point of view.

There seemed to be there a strong suggestion of another 'self', not expressed, and regretted.

Me: Can you describe a lesson when you felt you did take more of a part?

Jo: Well, in drama, it's split up into two groups, one who enjoys taking part and one who don't, and there were two of us who had to do one piece, and Mrs B picked out me and picked out someone from the other group who I didn't really get on with, and we did this piece together, just the two of us, in front of the whole class, and we did it really good, really well—and I thought, that was really great, I wish I could do it all the time.

Me: That's very interesting, can you say exactly what you felt?

Jo: I just felt I'd achieved something, because I felt, if I had to do it in front of the whole class then I'd just crack up and do everything wrong, so I just felt I'd achieved something.

Me: Yes.

Jo: Just felt—just felt really good.

Me: How did other people react to you?

Jo: (small pause) They thought it was very good as well (slight self-deprecating laugh)—they sort of came up and congratulated me—

Me: And did that feel good?

Jo: Yes (emphatically).

Me: Have you followed it up by doing the same again?

Jo: No (same laugh).

Me: Perhaps you will. Why did you make the choice of drama?

Jo: Umm—when I was younger I always wanted to be an actress and I just thought I'll do drama, because it's something I used to want to do. I just wanted to see if I'd enjoy it, because it's a lesson where you can sort of—get on with the other people—because it's not like another lesson, because when you're in that room [a very well-appointed studio] it's like another world, you can speak more freely in drama because everyone's on the same level . . .

The way I interpret what Joanne is saying is this:

She chose drama in the hope that the suppressed self—long since abandoned—of 'Joanne the confident assertive actress' could come out of hiding. It seems to me especially important that she talks of drama as 'another world'—and *not* the one in which she has had to accept her premature secretarihood. It was also a world in which 'everyone's on the same level' so that you can 'speak more freely'. These words suggest that for Joanne the expectation that everyone should speak, and act, meant that for the first time speaking out was a possibility, because she was *allowed* to escape from the self which for the rest of the time imprisoned her in silence.

Once again, there is a suggestion of the power of play to release from restrictive self-perception. It is as if she saw and understood that power—even though for most of the time in drama she did not use it, but remained on the sidelines, overawed, slightly frightened. It is as if she saw that her freedom might announce itself, if she could just find the right role to use; and that drama was her chance to try to find it.

I should have asked her what the piece was that she acted. But what is certain is that for those brief moments she spoke, she stood up, she proclaimed the importance of her own voice. And all acclaimed her. The fluency of her description, combined with slight incoherence, suggest how important this experience was; she'd feared, still trapped in secretarihood, that she'd crack up, but she didn't.

But as a key moment, a key opportunity, it was lost.

I interviewed her drama teacher. She made no mention of Joanne's performance, and said that she tended to be a watcher rather than a joiner; and would always end up in improvisations with the most unobtrusive roles.

Is it possible that this lost opportunity was critical—the point when a steady decrease of contentment might have been reversed? The danger for the passive and quiet is that signs they may show of loss of contentment, or of previously unsuspected ability, will tend to be vague and fleeting; and teachers' habit of inattention to someone so firmly relegated may anyway guarantee that those signs are not seen.

I suspect that her drama teacher did not notice Joanne's moment, because it did not fit with what she assumed Joanne to be. *She had already discounted her:* so she neutralized and blurred her attention when Joanne came to perform.

What does Joanne's story tell us about what may await Mona? If Mona is likely to become Joanne, then I foresee a steady loss of the sufficiency of her contentment. Many girls become good busy little workers; and for a while the reward of satisfying adults—and ensuring that their demands are not excessive nor their attention too intrusive—adds a nice polish to the pleasure of being busy and tidy. But as Mona becomes Joanne, a sense of dissatisfaction will grow until— perhaps—she dimly senses that the smiling adults who have let her go her own way *have never really been interested in her.*

Joanne at 16 seemed vaguely disappointed; mysteriously bereft. Mona's teachers were not interested in her, but in Liz and Darren and Frances and Nevin. Joanne's teachers didn't notice her much either and were content that she would became a 'bank girl', and had settled into her bank-girl personality.

It may be too late for Joanne. The theory she has acquired for herself may be the only one she will have for use in her life. Its returns will diminish and diminish; unless she is as lucky as Kerry.

Kerry

Like David and like Anne, Kerry's salvation came when her discontent grew and became so profound that she had to find an end to it.

To begin with, towards the end of her time in school, she accepted failure as her fate. She does not recall having had much power over her life at this time:

I don't remember ever having a choice. They put boys in for boys' subjects like physics, and so on, and girls in for girls' subjects. But I did enjoy biology.

She did poorly in her fourth-year work in this subject, and when she did well in the exam, she was accused of cheating. Her teachers could not believe that their relegation had been inaccurate.

I've done quite well in biology here. I got an A in O level.

Kerry was at David's FE college. She left school early, with no qualifica- tions, encouraged to do so by her father, with only one teacher speaking against him. But:

I wasn't fussed one way or the other. I don't know why. Nobody had told me that if you don't get exams, you can't get a good job, no one had pointed that out, so I left with nothing.

I finally got a job as a telephonist. I did that for two years, and then I got married, and then I got divorced; then I went to work for my father, then I couldn't stand that any more and I ended up here.

I asked her why she decided to go to the college.

I've got a young daughter, so I can't really do a full-time job, and I was bored out of my mind. I couldn't do any part-time job of any value because I had no qualifications, so I thought I'd use this time, now, to get some. When she's a bit older, I'll be able to go to university, and then get a decent job.

When she started, she set her sights very low.

I'd got this very negative attitude of myself, and when I came here, I applied to do remedial reading and maths, English and maths, I mean, and he [the first teacher she went to] convinced me to try for O level. And I've done it! I got an A, two B's and a C. Now I'm doing three A levels.

How was it, I asked, that her school failed to judge her accurately.

It wasn't really interested in the girls. There were very few girls doing sciences, and they were all talking about being private secretaries. We did cooking. The head was very dominant. He wanted girls to look pretty. There were two types of blouses and two types of blazers. I can remember the emphasis on that more than I can remember talk about exams and things like that. Socks till the third year, tights after that . . .

She talked more about her life as a young mother:

I was in a council estate, a massive one, right at the top of a hill. Pushing a pram up it was hell, and I didn't have that many friends. But I moved and then it got slightly better and then I thought what can I do? I was still very bored and depressed, but when I came here, it was really different, it was a new world—

It is interesting that both Anne and Paul made the same comment about their arrival at the college.

I felt I wasn't using my brain at all. I know lots of people far cleverer than me, with no qualifications doing dreadful jobs.

Kerry, then, is Joanne dumped in adult life, not having found out much about herself; and with so meagre an idea of her own capacity that when she first applies to the college, she asks for extra 'remedial' reading and maths. But she finds the college 'really different—a new world'. Its newness is to do with her finally meeting expectations which do in some way reflect her potential.

It is possible that her predicament in school would now be far less common—though by no means unknown. It is probably harder now for a head teacher to be so outrageously patronizing as hers was to girls. But my time in Mona's middle school showed me that though open discrimination may well be now less common in schools, a covert equivalent is as active as ever.

Somehow Mona and Joanne ought to be offered the opportunity to try out different ideas of what they might be. If they are not, Kerry's depression may be waiting for them; and who is to say whether they will be lucky and brave enough to make the journey to a college?

Education should not—for anyone, no matter what their ability—be a training in douce assiduity. Education should promote the active use of the mind, not its passive contented browsing. What Mona needed was to be benignly traumatized rather than benignly neglected: to be astonished and amazed and delighted and intrigued; to have her curiosity freed of its nice habits and frilly clothes and good manners, and returned to its original greed.

For one thing is certain. The sort of learning her school was offering Mona was encouraging her to find pleasure and reward in the fatuous virtues of neatness and keeping busy. For all but the privileged few, who won acknowledgement from their teachers, the 'work' they were doing was far too unstimulating.

It is to a discussion of the sort of learning of which I was an observer that I now want to turn.

CHAPTER EIGHT

Learning in Nomansland: Ginger

LET us now return to the middle school, and Class 4B.

Ginger was a small boy with ginger hair, and a very expressive face. When he was with his mates—boys whose contacts with teachers were fairly frequent, but mostly punitive in nature—the conversation he had with them made his face fill with fun, amazement, scorn, hilarity. He was very neatly built, with neat hands and neat quick movements; though in PE, in which most of the boys seemed at ease, he did not shine.

When he was talking to his friends, or playing complex and discreet games with them, he seemed intelligent and resourceful and shrewd. I saw him, for instance, enliven an art and craft lesson in which he was sewing initials on cloth, by stalking and killing a friend, again and again and again. Movement was legitimate; so Ginger, taking advantage of the teacher's absorption in another pupil's work, would move in quick unseen stages nearer and nearer his friend, who would never see him approach. Finally, he would enjoy a moment of silent anticipation. Then, judging his moment skilfully, he would pounce, and stab his friend in the kidneys with a forefinger, or chop the back of his neck with the side of his hand.

I never once saw him show any interest in a lesson. The ingenuity with which he managed to avoid his teachers' attention was very impressive. But though he seemed to have eyes in the back of his head, sometimes he grew too excited by whatever he was doing to kill time, and would forget the need to hide and dissemble—and a teacher would catch him out.

What would then happen would be the delivery of a reprimand, combined with attention to his work. More often than not, he would be told that he had not done enough, and asked what he had been doing. This question would never get a satisfactory answer, and he would be sent back to his seat, and told not to waste any more time. Teachers thus killed two birds with one stone: they administered the needed rebuke, and at the same time had a look at his work. But because this was the *only* sort of attention that he received, it was not something Ginger welcomed or wished to repeat. In other words, he associated attention with reprimand and irritated exhortation: 'don't waste any more time'.

The only contact he had with teachers was designed, each time, to drive home more and more firmly that education was unrewarding, painful, futile, punitive. He and his teachers were fixed in a ritual, in which their relations seemed to have become entirely predictable.

Ginger had not learned that to hide successfully, he must not only answer questions, keep his eyes well down, and make himself as unattractive as possible, but he must also never allow himself to be seen doing deviant and unacceptable things, and always be seen being busy. However, I felt that there was too much life in him, too much capacity for excitement and enjoyment, for him ever to learn that lesson successfully. He would always be caught out.

He presented no problems to his teachers at all, so he could be safely ignored until his antics broke loose from their usual discretion and he became unavoidably noticeable. As a 'lazy bad boy', he was ignored and relegated: the equivalent of the nice silent girls. It is hard to decide whose predicament was worse.

This child's imprisonment in a self-defeating pattern of behaviour—which, unless it stopped, could only lead to greater disenchantment, boredom, and dissociation of school from pleasure—seemed so complete, so ineluctable a fact, that it was very hard to imagine it coming to an end.

But how had it begun?

Perhaps, with great haphazardness, through a process in which a number of factors might have combined. His parents' dismissive attitude to education, possibly; an early 'bad' relationship with a teacher who couldn't help disliking him, and pushed him into acquiring a strategy of evasion; a habit of slight fear of adults learnt from a violent father and an unpredictable mother; a difficulty in concentrating because of never having learnt to associate pleasure with school.

One could speculate endlessly. But less speculative is the likelihood that at no time in the eight years in which this process developed was there a conscious and subtle attempt to intervene and reverse it. His relegation felt as if it had been established for years.

What Ginger's teachers were doing was—as I watched—so familiar, that it seemed in no way remarkable. But to think of it in retrospect is to realize how extraordinary it was. Here was a boy of 13, faculties intact, being abandoned to educational failure. I have suggested that when teachers begin to express a pious hope that things will change, they have abandoned the pupil they see as in need of change. Roger was immature; so Mrs Roberts had to wait for him to ripen. Ginger was an 'idle little nuisance', or some such figment; and all his teachers seemed to be able to do was wait for him to turn into Frances or Liz.

Teachers are for ever awaiting the miraculous, which accounts per-haps for the air of perpetual disappointment worn by some of them.

What could, or should, they have done? One, or two, or *all* of his teachers could have made it their deliberate business to acknowledge him. They could, at least, have sat down together to talk about him, and try to work out some strategy for his 'rescue'.

This, of course, is what all the witnesses I have called needed at some point in their school career: deliberation and discussion leading to planned change. The strategy for Ginger would be first to put an end to all the negative, retributive attention they were giving him: to take him off the medicine that was making him hate school. Then there should have followed a wilful attempt to include him in every lesson and every activity, and to acknowledge all his efforts and contributions.

In other words, taking him by surprise, they should have completely reversed their meagre expectations of him, and transformed their way of approaching him. But in schools as I have known them, teachers are neither asked, nor do they have time, to scrutinize the complexities of their pupils' predicaments—unless those pupils are making unacceptable demands on them.

They do not like it when learning stops: they want all their pupils to learn. But when it does stop, all they seem to be able to do is fish out a soiled old statement like 'work harder'—or in Ginger's case 'stop wast-ing time'. All they seem to be able to do is hope for change, and apply the futile poultice of vague exhortation.

What they also could not do was construct a way of learning that *in itself* would offer an opportunity of reversing Ginger's habit of evasion. For Ginger was bored; and his boredom was the best guarantor of his evasion and his relegation.

It seemed to me that what he and his classmates were being asked to do was of a nature that encouraged passivity—or, rather, made it inevit-able that many—like Mona—would be driven to the trivial pleasures of business and tidiness as a way of making the unrewarding bearable—just as a prisoner in solitary confinement fends off despair with obsessive routines.

It seemed that the pedagogy itself—to use the jargon word—conspired with other culpable influences in her life to make Mona find solace in neat handwriting and a nimbly wielded ruler; it seemed that the daily intellectual diet was itself so boring that Ginger could see no reason for ending his disenchantment.

Inactivity in class

During lessons, many pupils gave the appearance of wanting to escape: wanting to be absent when present, like Ginger. There were several, like Liz, who seemed to have accepted study as a profitable pursuit, one that engaged them fully—though they, as I shall show, were favoured by their teachers in ways that made this likely.

But even Liz and her like sometimes suffered with the rest. She looked as bowed down as anyone when she went into her current affairs class and had to listen to a long monologue about the history of parliament; or when another harangue on hygiene commenced from Mrs Phillips.

So much of what they were asked to do was uninteresting because they were not being asked to be sufficiently active. I find it impossible to listen passively for very long to anyone lecturing, however excited I am by his subject—and I am in my thirties with an excitable mind, used to receiving ideas and information. After a while I want to talk, to question, to handle for myself the ideas and facts being presented to me—just as someone who is having a new device presented wants to try it for himself, rather than listen endlessly to a description of how it works.

Moreover, when they *were* asked to be active, there was seldom any doubt about the outcome of the activity concerned. To do an exercise from 'the book' in French or science, was, as the word 'exercise' suggests, routine, familiar, and predictable—and could make no appeal to curiosity. Now, such routine work is an inevitable part of learning. It cannot be made to disappear. But such work should always be servant to an enterprise that *does* appeal to curiosity, and not an end in itself. Far too much of what I saw suggested that exercises are the essence of education, rather than a subsidiary necessity.

Curiosity is a state of not knowing, and wanting to find out. It thrives on the possession of a certain amount of information, and the pursuit of more in order to throw light on a problem or mystery that the original information has no power to illumine.

When taught, you can *want* to understand, to satisfy your curiosity, or you can be *told* to understand. In the lessons I saw, pupils were on the whole being told to understand, and to practise what they'd been told to understand. This is what it is, this is how you do it, these are the exercises that will help you to master how to do it. Now do them, and master it. Why? Because I tell you to, that's why.

A small child wants to understand because it is engaged in exploration of its world. All the time it meets mysteries. It wants to understand those mysteries, so that it can take its exploration further, and make sense of the next tract of territory it meets. Exploration is exciting and daunting and active. It is risky, and deeply satisfying.

But what I saw was older children, not being asked to explore new territory, led authoritatively by knowledgeable teachers, but being forced, instead, to march across it with their heads down.

Consider Ginger, whom I watched during one lesson maintain undetected a conversation about fishing, with his neighbour, for almost half an hour. Ginger, who was cleverer at putting off teachers than anyone else; who, when a teacher asked him to bring his work to the front to be looked at, would make himself so uninteresting with his monosyllabic answers, his refusal to smile or raise his eyes, that he would soon be sent back to his mates to get on with whatever he was doing to break the law and make the time pass more quickly. Ginger, who, when questions were being asked around the class, would duck his head and stay resolutely still.

Consider the subjects Ginger was learning. In maths, the routine was to sit and 'do questions' from the book. Occasionally, something would be explained on the board ('this is how it's done; now practise it . . .'). Occasionally his exercise book would be looked at, condemned, and returned—so that for a while he would march more quickly.

In French, there was homework—reading something new about the Duponts, learning some words, and doing some exercises. In class there were tests, more questions, and reading more instalments about the life of the Duponts.

In history, the diet could be leavened by, for instance, watching a film strip. But even that seemed all too like watching television, and led only to desultory discussion, in which the leaders of talk dominated, as usual. Otherwise, it was reading the book, listening to the teacher, and writing essays and answers to questions in the book.

Geography was the 'project': copying stuff from library books. This subject was taught by an agreeable, friendly, warm man, who also taught PE, and had a knack of encouraging even the most obviously unathletic to enjoy themselves—though Ginger, as I have said, was an exception here.

In science, again, 'the book' predominated. Practicals there must have been; but in two weeks all I saw was 'the book', and questions, and a certain amount of explanation, and discussion dominated by the talkative, participating minority; and, of course, long private discussions between the teacher and Liz, in which I suspect her curiosity was successfully answered and successfully kept alive.

At nine-thirty one morning, I note, during the teacher's routine examination of homework—questions from the book, to be answered neatly:

Teacher to Ginger to check his homework. Pantomime (mild) on Ginger's face as he says he hasn't done it—a smile concealed behind a poor attempt at humble apology, his head ducked. Teacher moves away after absolutely minimal contact with Ginger, whereas with B and Ro, just before and just after, he spent longer.

Ten minutes later, I record that Ginger is talking animatedly to his neighbour. I also note, beside my record of contacts:

In all this perambulation (while class is working, from book), T is responding to kids' demands for attention, rather then choosing someone to visit whom he judges in need of attention.

So that Ginger, chatting, is safe.

Religious education: a book, a text read for homework, questions round the class (guess who answers them?) a long lecture on the subject of the next chapter.

Health education: harangues, the book, homework based on the book; harangues; respite: do your own poster on tooth decay.

In none of this was Ginger asked to be active, in the sense of positively satisfying his curiosity; doing something of intellectual or imaginative importance to him, the outcome of which was not pre-ordained.

All his ingenious methods of passing the time were active. His stalking was a beautiful example: intelligence, guile and agility were engaged, as was his hunter's vigilance in case he too were being hunted. And his judgement of the moment when his stealth had succeeded and he could pounce, was a piece of refined and brilliantly speedy deliberation. He had to know that others were not watching him, and would not give him away; had to be sure that the teacher's attention was still safely elsewhere; had to be sure that his stealthy feet were still—at this last crucial moment—inaudible to his victim.

And yet, such inspired activity, such intelligence, I saw being used only for his own distraction, and never for what he should have been doing. His relegation was completely successful, his disenchantment probably irreversible—because none of what he was being asked to do was as appealing as stalking his friend and jabbing him in the ribs.

Stuffing

But it would not be just to blame the teachers for what they were offering Ginger and his classmates. Syllabuses are large; time is short. It is difficult for teachers not to put too much emphasis on acquiring information and too little on absorbing, enjoying, understanding. For teachers know that if their pupils can demonstrate that they know their *stuff*, something concrete will have been achieved. Knowing your stuff will guarantee a less than hopeless showing in an exam. Knowing your stuff, or seeming to know it, in the pieces of class-work that accumulate to a 'folder' in the New Order of continuous assessment will ensure a less than hopeless grade in GCSE. Understanding your stuff will mean a better showing; but possessing and exhibiting it in undigested form will at least be evidence that something has been achieved.

To encourage true learning is subtle and complex. Because of the inimical circumstances in which so much schoolteaching takes place, it is often easier and perhaps unavoidable to make stuffing a substitute for learning—with grave implications.

One is that industry can be promoted as a virtue in itself, rather than a necessary means to an end; and lack of industry, similarly, can be condemned as the great school sin.

Teachers can comfortably neglect Mona and Ginger and their like, so long as they acquire a minimum of stuff. If industrious stuffing is one of the purposes of being in school, pupils who stuff—even as little as Ginger stuffed—can be left. There is no reason why GCSE, unaided by changes in circumstances, will necessarily alter this feature of life in Nomansland.

There is too little pressure on teachers to discriminate between different sorts of industry—because any industry implies that stuff is being acquired. Industry is also, of course, an aid to good order, and always to be welcomed for that reason too.

For some, however, stuffing is less deadly.

Acknowledgement and stuffing

The acknowledged, like Liz, are more likely to be actively engaged in the pursuit of knowledge to satisfy their curiosity than pupils like Ginger. Their teachers are excited by their excitement, and seek to feed it. As the rest of the platoon is prodded and dragged across the terrain of Education, they, the acknowledged, walk beside their teachers, who keep pointing out interesting features, and answer their interested questions about what lies ahead.

The acknowledged, heads lifted, constantly see things they have never seen before; and if they do not notice them, their teachers will point them out. The rest, heads bowed, see only the ground, their feet, the book; see only what they know and can predict.

For teachers, though they may let many or most of their pupils get their heads down and learn their stuff, know that helping pupils to understand, to be curious, and to find intellectual and imaginative pleasure—is far more rewarding than just giving them stuff to learn and write. While encouraging large numbers of their pupils to believe that stuffing is enough, teachers subversively seek out the most confident, curious, and excitable (but *not* necessarily the most able) to acknowledge them, and give them their special attention.

The pressure of large syllabuses and the hunt for credentials force this division between the acknowledged and what Jane called the 'just taught'. Teachers are forced to escape these and other constraints by seeking pupils with whom they can transcend them.

These allies, these acknowledged ones, will not only be the beneficiaries of their teachers' unregenerate desire to make some pupils understand and enjoy; but their stuffing will constantly be spiced by purpose and pleasure. Small children want stuff—seek information—because it helps them to make sense of the world. Making sense is for them both exciting and rewarding, and as vital as food. Information thus serves their need, their craving. The acknowledged are encouraged by their teachers to continue to find excitement and reward in *making sense*.

For so many of the industrious relegated, the rewards of industry are red ticks, mild smiles, and neglect. But for the lucky ones, industry itself becomes an aid to understanding and delight. It becomes a chosen activity: I will learn this stuff because it will enhance my understanding and give me pleasure. For the relegated, stuffing is either a passively accepted necessity, or a chance to practise their prisoners' skills of neatness, niceness, and nimbleness.

Liz and science

A science lesson I watched was very interesting in this connection. The difference between the way the teacher was teaching Liz, and the rest of the class, was—as I have already suggested—considerable. On this occasion, the subject of the lesson was classification: the usefulness of arranging things in classes which denote some defined similarity between those things—some shared essential.

No doubt it was laid down by the syllabus that before this class went to senior school, they should know about classification. In other words, they should know what it means, understand how the idea of classification works, and be able to apply it.

There was a chapter in the book about classification. The lesson began with this chapter—the text of which was brief—being read. The teacher had already drawn, meticulously and with great skill, a sheep, a goat, a cow; and on the other side of the board, a shirt, a pair of trousers, a skirt, and a pair of shoes. Using the participators to help him, he explained, again, the basic notion of classification already unfolded by the book. He then gave more examples of things and the classes into which they could be put.

In this part of the lesson he was extremely skilful: he spoke clearly, his drawings were excellent, and the time he gave to each piece of explanation was well judged. Then he told the class to do the questions, which were modest and undemanding exercises in classification, demanding a minimum of thought.

So far then, a text had been read, the class had been lectured, and now they were to show that they had been paying attention.

Soon Liz was at the teacher's table—this was the lesson when I recorded that she spent ten minutes with him—and they were to be seen talking animatedly. I heard odd snatches of questions, deliveries of praise and enthusiasm. 'How would you classify . . .?' I heard once; and though I was not near enough to hear their conversation in detail, I would guess that much of it had the nature of the posing and solution of problems. At one point, I know, they were talking about flowers. Their conversation was also, I noticed with great interest, full of pauses when Liz was given the luxury of being allowed to think.

If my guess is right, then Liz was being put in a position where she was experimenting with the usefulness of classification: being given, and tackling, problems which gave her intellectual experience of its function. She was obviously interested; and any subsequent work—and any stuff—involving classification would be illumined and given meaning by their conversation.

A good educational experience

Liz's teacher was leading her authoritatively through a good educational experience. Rather than guiding her, or prompting her own discoveries, he was much more dominant and in command: he was navigating her progress and her pleasure.

The distinction is important. I am not advocating an agricultural programme of education, in which the child is left to browse happily in a field she chooses, while all that her teacher does is point out where the best grass grows, and suggest where she might go to find another good field. I am talking about a teacher leading her pupil—as a parent leads her child—to experiences she knows are vital if her child is to learn mastery of her world, and is to continue to find pleasure in acquiring mastery. A parent does not, for instance, let her untutored child find its own— blissfully discovering—way to the pleasure of painting. A parent buys paints and paper and shows her child how to use them. She suggests colours, ideas, techniques, which she knows will be fruitful. She leads; but she does not dictate. She suggests; but she does not impose. She is authoritative rather than authoritarian, and acknowledges the progress her child makes, delighting in its smallest achievement.

The relationship between learner and taught thus depicted is a collaboration in which one party has greater knowledge and experience, which she uses with wisdom and authority for the benefit of the other.

Liz was lucky to be enjoying such a relationship. But for most of the rest of the class, there were no problems, no conversations in which thought was provoked and insight praised. A text was read, the teacher talked, and some pitifully simple exercises were done. I was sitting near Ginger and a friend, and they managed to get through the exercises competently enough, while chattering away and discreetly assaulting each other—and very occasionally putting pen to paper.

Liz was actively engaged, and Frances and some of the boys, including Darren, were given a little private tuition at the table—though none enjoyed such long and elaborate exchanges as Liz's. Other pupils appeared at the table—but only to have their books glanced at. The rest were passively going through simple motions having been doled out the relevant stuff. Yet *all* members of that class were entitled to Liz's experience.

It is possible to say that in teaching a few, and Liz in particular, this teacher was doing his job well. I am certain that he was an extremely effective private tutor: the favoured pupils went back for more; while with him their interest was unmistakable, as was his enthusiasm. And many of the pupils who were left to swim unaided did, I am sure, steadily increase their knowledge, and were embarked on a course that would end with modest success in science. But modest success in examinations is not the same as being interested in the subject concerned, or being educated in it. Who knows how many of the pupils I watched would have benefited from acknowledgement, and developed an interest to last them all their lives—achieving more startling results in the process?

How many true Nomanslanders among them had potential that was never glimpsed and was never to develop; but who, as long as they got on with their stuff throughout their school careers, could be thought of as modest successes?

The division between the taught and the rest may well endure, despite changes associated with GCSE; and it is far from implausible to suggest that in GCSE there will materialize different sorts of passes: that those who pass well will have benefited from teachers' time, and have been encouraged to make the most of the imaginative, participatory work GCSE seeks to promote; and that those whose passes are ordinary will at least have convinced their assessors that they know some stuff.

Too many pupils spend most of their schooling doing the equivalent of 'colouring in'. They're given the outlines and the shapes and a simple code for the colours to use, and they're told what it is will appear when the colours have all been applied. Or, rather, what they're given are not those clever puzzles in which a hidden shape appears, but uncoloured shapes the identity of which is stunningly obvious. Different shapes for different objects; but the same process each time, which in the end deadens, clouds, depresses, frustrates.

What do they *not* learn? To solve problems, to take initiative, to explore and elaborate an idea; to struggle to understand something because understanding is itself a pleasure; to listen to ideas not their own, which help their own ideas to develop.

A brief glimpse of more active learning

I did witness an interesting English lesson. The teacher, Mrs S, had divided the class into four groups. During the previous lesson, she had read them half of a story in which two boys, exploring a bit of sea-shore, get separated. Meanwhile the tide is coming in. The task was for each group to decide what was going to happen next. They had to discuss their ideas, and then a spokesperson would report to the whole class on their discussion.

What they were asked to do was active, collaborative, and creative. Most important of all, the outcome of what they were doing was not decided. A certain amount of information was given; and curiosity and imagination had to get to work on that information, and take it further.

I noted that the usually more articulate tended to dominate discussion in the groups, and that four habitual non-responders seemed to get away with saying nothing at all. But I also noted two other identified non-responders having their ideas at least canvassed by the more vocal; and the teacher wandering from group to group was able to prod the more reticent herself. It certainly seemed that it was less easy for members of Nomansland to elude and evade in small groups than in a whole class.

The spokespersons were without exception the more vocal and responsive. The ideas they reported were delightfully varied. Someone had one of the boys meet a mermaid who, he stressed, had very long black hair; and there were many subtle reasons why one of them might have got lost, as well as dramatic accounts of one of the boys being cut off by the rising tide, on a rock.

The atmosphere during the time allocated for discussion felt so different from the dreary feeling of so many of the lessons I had watched. From time to time the teacher had to ask for less noise because people were getting carried away by their eagerness to make their own suggestions about what had happened. It seemed that more were engaged and interested than not—even though some, whose demeanour in school was firmly and consistently passive, remained outside the excitement.

After the reports were over, Mrs S read the rest of the story; and for the first half of the next lesson she went over points of grammar, vocabulary and style that had arisen.

What I had seen was very interesting for a number of reasons. First, it was a different sort of mental exercise from any I had seen in other lessons. The children, grouped and asked to invent, had no idea of the outcome of their discussions. They were creating the solution to a problem. The problem had been put to them with clarity and force. Mrs S was an extremely good reader, and her suggestion of various important features of the problem—the tide rising, the inexperience of the boys, their excitement—was nicely judged to heighten interest. So the pupils were being put into a position for which school should provide training: facing and tackling a metal task with energy and optimism; actively trying to master a problematic proposition.

In the lesson on classification, all information was given; and the pupils were asked to put the information to work in set and predictable ways. The most 'problematic' of the questions they were asked was to find the odd man out in a list of things belonging to a particular class. The culprits were, to say the least, not hard to identify—on the lines of: cabbage, lettuce, cauliflower, giraffe.

The pupils had no control of this activity. It was not theirs, but the book's. The issue of classification certainly could have been presented in a way that allotted to them an enquiry and a set of problems to make their own and solve for themselves.

Let us say—to use a modest example, and one which would not have been time-consuming to contrive, for teachers have very little time— that a room or stock cupboard had been, deliberately, slightly untidied for pupils; and that, three by three, they had been asked to go into that room to list its contents, without being told why they were being asked to do so.

When they returned with their lists of unclassified things—eight canes, ten Bibles, four set-squares, one tambourine (no bells)—would have been the moment for judicious introduction of information, and the idea of classification. Not only would such a sequence have asked for open and unpredictable activity—militating against passive digestion, repetition, browsing—but it would have been a minute piece of training in independent mastery of the world, rather than submissive, acquiescent rehearsal of a text already written and glossed by the authorities of Book and Teacher.

In form, too, this approach would have suggested that information and knowledge exist to serve and enhance independent mastery; and that known science connects to the real world of disordered cupboards. So that subsequent information, when it came, would be made sense of by them as well as by their teacher. Zoology needs classification just like that cupboard does, would be their modest revelation.

Just so did Mrs S introduce her many and rigorous points about grammar, spelling and punctuation *after* pupils had been asked to try to put themselves on an equal footing with the writer of the story, becoming all the more eager to find out how *she* ended it for having tried themselves, and all the more appreciative of her skill and ingenuity as a result; all the more critical, too, perhaps believing that some of their ideas might have been an improvement. (I should have added that for homework, between lessons, all had to write their own ending of the story.)

There was another crucial difference between these two lessons. Mrs S, grouping her pupils, asked them to work together. One of the most woeful features of many of the lessons I watched was the privacy of the pupils' inactivity and boredom. Doing work from the book is a training in passivity, which only the attractive and confident can alleviate by luring their teachers into acknowledging them and awarding them the privilege of real teaching. But for those inclined to passivity, or wanting anonymity and escape, work secures their imprisonment, as does the expectation that they will plod through their work alone.

The important feature of Mrs S's lesson was that, although in the groups the lively tended to dominate, the passive *did* contribute—if in a small way—and *were* appealed to in the discussions, rather than never being asked questions and never asking them.

This has important implications. Their thoughts were thus awarded validity which their normal reticence denied them; and it was much more difficult *not* to express their thoughts than it normally would have been.

But my chief feeling after watching this English lesson was that if you give pupils responsibility for their own work, giving them mysteries and difficulties which they have to solve—you can expect energy, excitement, and unsolicited seriousness; a seriousness which extends to the articulate rescuing the evasive from their isolation.

Most important of all, it seemed to me, was that I had witnessed a lesson in which many more pupils than usual talked, purposefully and at length.

Mastery and talk

The importance of collaboration in learning—and by collaboration I mean, essentially, discussing work with others—is that it promotes mastery rather than passive reception, by means of talk. You master information and ideas when you talk about them; and when your writing about them is not regurgitation or slavish exercise, but an expression of what you have—internally or aloud—said.

This is not to say that mastery is originality: that it is only when a pupil makes a unique statement that proper learning is taking place. Rather it is to say that, until you speak a thought, silently or vocally, it will not be yours, but someone else's—the book's or the teacher's.

In a discussion in which A says to B, 'You mean that it was the stirrup that made charges on horseback possible because you could hold on well enough to carry and use a lance?', A is asking if she may lawfully make her formulation of a fact truly her own.

When B says, 'You've got it!', A has become the proud owner of knowledge rather than its passive borrower, colourer-in, or copier. To the extent that she has re-created knowledge in her own way, so that she says, 'Oh, I see!', to the same extent has she mastered it.

I am equating, or connecting, three things: understanding, talk, and re-creation. Ginger is going short of all three. He is not talking about his work; he is not truly understanding his work; because he is not making it his own. All he is doing is producing marks on paper to appease adults who bore him.

Re-creation

The word interests me. To stuff for an exam so that you can parade your stuff when the time comes, is to borrow information which you will then hand back to oblivion. But if you have *spoken* that stuff in energetic discourse, or inner revelation, or in argumentative essays, it will be yours. You will have re-created it for yourself.

The higher you attain in education, the more you are asked, in exams or aloud, to talk, to discuss. What distinguishes the 'educated'? Not the quantity of stuff stored in their minds, but the ability to discriminate between a poor and a sound argument; the ability to 'state with reasons'; the ability to discuss conflicting issues and decide priorities; the ability, above all, to *articulate*.

The higher you reach, in both arts and sciences, the more essays you must tackle which ask you to *discuss*. The essay, tyrant to stuffers, pleasure to those whose habit has been to discuss, to re-create ideas and information for themselves—the essay is an exercise in talking.

I believe that, for most people, the only way to learn to talk on paper—to learn, indeed, to think—is to talk aloud. Those who do not talk in school, to each other or to their teachers (and if not to either, then almost certainly not learning the art and pleasure of talking to themselves), may fail to acquire the skill that is most crucial for the continuation of their education.

Adolescents do not want to be skilled copyists, bored repeaters. They want to use their minds, and actively seek to master their world. The impulse to go on being as curious and engaged as children of early primary school age is not the natural monopoly of the gifted or attractive, or of boys like Darren who have found confidence enough to enjoy the limelight. It becomes their monopoly, because they tend to monopolize the opportunities for communication and collaboration: for useful talk.

This is perhaps the main reason why Liz was likely to do well, and Ginger was likely to fail; why the girls who hardly ever spoke would be unlikely to go very far.

Teachers enjoy teaching the communicative more than the evasive. Their enjoyment, their appreciation, expresses their awareness of the importance of talk—of communication.

Which pupils teachers like teaching

I carried out long interviews with twenty-eight teachers in the comprehensive school I have already mentioned. My task, chiefly, was to ask them to talk about the girls in the fourth year they had ticked on the list of names I had sent them all, as being 'quiet, compliant, biddable, hard to get to know'. But I also asked them questions of general interest to me. The most productive of these questions was: 'What sort of pupils do you on the whole like teaching most?'

Five did not commit themselves. Three said, 'the brightest'. One teacher, who I had reason to suspect was gifted at her work, said, 'the most difficult, because they challenge me'. Three others made interesting statements—such as to say, in one case, that he liked 'self-motivated kids'.

The other seventeen, in various ways, said that they like teaching those whom *they do engage*—who were not, they made clear, necessarily the most able. Those who communicate; those they acknowledge, and who respond. They like, variously:

The ones who initially find it a bit difficult, but then after a bit say, 'Ah yes, I've got it—'

Like everyone, I suppose, the ones who respond most obviously to me and the few that you make a breakthrough with.

You work on them, you try to acknowledge them, and finally they reciprocate.

Kids I have to work on, then suddenly it comes through.

Ones who struggle but in the end achieve.

The ones I enjoy teaching most are some of the less bright ones who still work, still try, and do get something.

Any child who will respond to what I'm doing.

And how about this one, for the importance of talk:

The ones who have got a brightness about them, who have plenty of questions.

I want people who have willingness to learn. I like people best who match my enthusiasm. [Those who talk, who smile and attract, who collaborate with her enthusiasm . . .]

The ones who do communicate with me.

Any who are excited or interested.

I like a bit of twinkle and spark from them.

The ones obviously [why is it obvious?] who are motivated, who are interested in language, who want to learn.

All these statements either suggest or state that pupils are favoured who communicate, and who join in. It is interesting, too, that four teachers mention the delight of 'breakthrough', of pupils who suddenly get something, and pupils who do respond to attempts to acknowledge them.

Theirs seem to me the clearest statements that pupils are favoured who communicate with their teachers. Moments of breakthrough—whether of sudden intellectual certainty, or a child's sudden response to attempts to acknowledge her or him, after long resistance—are moments of communication at its purest and most gratifying.

So, those teachers, when they talked about what they found most rewarding, indicated the importance of contact with their pupils; implied the importance of their pupils talking; suggested strongly that for them, conversation is the most important instrument of teaching. They may spend far too much of their time lecturing—or hectoring; they may be trapped by syllabuses and exam requirements into spending far too much time doling out information in easily digestible forms; but the times they look forward to, the times they treasure, are those occasions when they can communicate freely with their acknowledged pupils, with the members of their 'families'.

I feel that these teachers were confirming my suspicion that in most classrooms, two sorts of teaching take place: the genuine, passionate, enthusiastic article that her science teacher awarded to Liz; and second-best for the rest.

Talk—release—acknowledgement

Teaching can itself be an experience of the vital part that talk can play in thought. On my teaching practice, I was given a bright A level class, studying eighteenth-century British political history. My degree was in history; but that period was one I'd neglected, because its complexities had baffled and overawed me. I did not find Augustan assurance and dislike of 'enthusiasm' to my taste, as a would-be revolutionary and a Coleridge-carrying romantic.

But I found that having to teach this period made it much more interesting. I was forced to be in command of material that had always before eluded me. I am sure that what gave me this new pleasure was that I had to articulate my ideas, and to make facts my own. I was forced to talk to myself, in order to be able to talk to my pupils. I spent much of my time muttering to the books I read, rather than stubbornly getting through them all, copying salient facts into my notebook, feeling always that I was being steadily defeated by a sullen subject I could not master.

Teaching made public my private discussions. What had been before private aversion to a period, became a collaborative pleasure in its complexities.

It is interesting that this experience of mine was of release: frustration and aversion ended when I began to have to think more clearly; and when I began to talk in order to think.

When I say that I talked to myself, I mean that to prepare the clarity I wanted to offer my pupils, I had to imagine them as I worked: I had to imagine talking to them, and I had to ensure that what I said was not ambiguous or confused. Talking to real pupils in lessons was a continuation of the conversations I had been having with myself.

This experience of release has the same *form* as what happens to those lucky enough to escape from Nomansland and begin a real education: many of my witnesses were released from silence into a new pleasure of talking.

The following article is an example of such help being successfully given to another sort of pupil altogether. Those concerned were making trouble for their teachers. It is interesting that an ingenious, time-consuming, and expensive experiment was contrived in order to help them; but I know of no such experiment being offered to the discreet refugees of Nomansland.

The best way to learn is to teach. This is the message emerging from experiments in several schools in which teenage pupils who have problems at school themselves are tutoring younger children—with remarkable results for both sides.

According to American research, pupil tutoring wins 'hands down' over computerised instruction and American teachers say that no other recent innovation has proved so consistently successful.

Now the idea is spreading in Britain. Throughout this term, a group of 14-year-olds at Trinity comprehensive in Leamington Spa have been spending an hour a week helping children at a nearby primary school with their reading. The younger children read aloud to their tutors (who are supervised by university students of education) and then play word games with them.

All the 14-year-olds have some of their own lessons in a special unit for children who have difficulties at school. Though their intelligence is around average, most of them have fallen behind on reading, writing and maths and, in some cases, this has led to truancy or bad behaviour in class.

Jean Bond, who is running the special unit while on sabbatical from Warwick University's education department, says that the main benefit of tutoring is that it improves the adolescents' self-esteem. 'The younger children come rushing up every time and welcome them. It makes the tutors feel important whereas, in normal school lessons, they often feel inadequate. Everyone benefits. The older children need practice in reading but, if they had to do it in their own classes, they would say it was kids' stuff and be worried about losing face. The younger children get individual attention from very patient people. The tutors are struggling at school themselves so, when the younger ones can't learn, they know exactly why.'

The tutors agree. 'When I was little, I used to skive and say I couldn't do things when really I could', says Mark Greger. 'The boy I've been teaching does the same. He says he can't read a page of his book so I tell him that, if he does do it, we can play a game. That works.'

The younger children speak warmly of their new teachers. 'He doesn't shout like other teachers', says eight-year-old Jenny of her tutor, Cliff McFarlane who, among his own teachers, has a reputation for being a handful. Yet Cliff sees himself as a tough teacher. 'If they get a word wrong', he says, 'I keep them at it until they get it right.'

Jean Bond, who describes pupil tutoring as an 'educational conjuring trick', has run two previous experiments. In one, six persistent truants, aged 15 upwards, tutored 12 slow-learning infants in reading and maths. None of the six played truant from any of the tutoring sessions. 'The degree of concentration they showed while working with their tutees was remarkable for pupils who had previously shown little ability to concentrate on anything related to school work for any period of time,' writes Bond in the current issue of Educational Review. The tutors became 'reliable, conscientious, caring individuals'.

Their own reading, previously mechanical and monotonous, became far more expressive as a result of reading stories aloud to infants. Their view of education, which they had previously dismissed as 'crap' and 'a waste of time', was transformed. They became firmly resolved to teach their own children to read before starting school because, as one of them put it, 'if they go for a job and they can't write, they're not going to employ you, are they?' The tutors also became more sympathetic to their own teachers' difficulties, because they were frustrated themselves when the infants 'mucked about'.

In the seven weeks of the experiment, concludes Bond, 'these pupils received more recognition, reward and feelings of worth than they had previously experienced in many years of formal schooling.' And the infants, according to their own teachers, showed measureable gains in reading skills by the end of the scheme.

Other experiments have shown clear gains in children's learning. Carol Fitz-Gibbon, a lecturer at Newcastle University, got low-achieving 14-year-olds in Los Angeles to teach fractions to nine-year-olds. After the experiment, the tutors did much better on a test than contemporaries who had been taught fractions in normal lessons. Even more remarkably, they maintained their lead on another test three months later, while the other children seemed to have forgotten everything they had learnt. 'The almost total lack of retained progress in the non-tutor group must have occurred routinely every year', writes Fitz-Gibbon in a report to the Social Science Research Council.

The experiment was repeated in England and, though the results were not as startling, they still suggested that pupil tutoring worked. Fitz-Gibbon reports that several tutors were anxious to get their sums right to save embarrassment in front of younger children. 'In low-achieving secondary maths classes it is frequently quite difficult to induce any sense of *needing* to learn maths. References to later employability or exam success mean little to restless teenagers. The tutoring project provided tutors with an *immediate* need to know the work.'

Advocates of pupil tutoring stress that it is essential for the tutors to be more advanced in reading and maths than the younger pupils. This is why tutoring within the same age group, or across a narrow age difference, does not work. They also point out that, unlike the 19th century monitorial system (when older children acted as cost-saving teachers) the new-style tutoring is anything but cheap. As well as organising the tutors' visits to primary schools, the teachers have to find time to brief them in detail and to supervise the tutoring sessions. But Jean Bond believes that the investment is worthwhile. 'It gives these children a taste of success', she says. 'And that's something they get far too little of.'

PETER WILBY
Sunday Times, 5 December 1982

© Times Newspapers Limited 1982

These unhappy 14-years-olds were evidently enjoying a similar experience to mine of teaching eighteenth-century history. When their pupils were encouraged to read, they were re-creating the words before them for someone equipped to tell them when their re-creation was accurate, so that they could be told, 'You've got it!'

These boys showed seriousness, too, when given responsibility for their work, and a chance to communicate and collaborate. They had to be in command of their material: they had to be able to talk—to read—clearly and authoritatively. Their experience of responsibility, of mastery, made their own reading improve greatly.

Perhaps what Ginger needed was to be turned into a teacher.

In large classes, too many pupils have too few chances to talk purposively about their work. These tutoring experiments gave people the opportunity to talk—above all—and to be released from private frustration. They exemplify, too, the importance of acknowledgement (note the implication that the acknowledgement the tutors offered was based on sound and thorough empathy, because the tutors knew from first-hand experience what their pupils' predicament was like. It was that accurate empathy that all my witnesses needed and so seriously lacked) and collaboration, as well as the importance of talk, communication. Pupil and tutor are actively engaged; and both gain. Working closely, they acknowledge each other.

One of the most moving passages in the article describes the welcome the tutors are given by their pupils—giving them a sense of validity and importance. This sense should be supplied to the tutors in their own work with their own classmates and their own teachers. Instead, falling behind in the race for credentials, relegated to 'difficult', and 'maladjusted' or 'disruptive'—there are many sorts of relegation—their experience of education is, like Ginger's, endlessly negative.

But the tutoring experiment helped to lift them out of self-contempt, and offered them a more generous idea of what they were and could be.

They were thus luckier than the inhabitants of Nomansland, on whom such ingenuity is never lavished.

A note on GCSE

Since education for 11- to 16-year-olds is changing with the arrival of GCSE, the above may be taken as a critique of the Old Order. But the Old Order is not just syllabuses and methods, but habits and beliefs as well. And the new has been introduced too quickly—with patchy preparation and perfunctory retraining. Most of the scant time available has been spent on the cobbling of courses, as GCSE to some extent allows schools to create their own. There has been too little time for persuasion, discussion, and for learning not just new methods but their purpose too. The result is that many teachers will go on much as before.

Worse is that there seems to have been little, if any, appreciation of the need for new conditions, as well as courses and methods. GCSE English, for instance, enshrines the sound principle that the ability to talk must be fostered and assessed. Teachers must now monitor that ability, as well as carry out other new sorts of assessment. But they are not provided with enough, if any, extra time to do these things; which leads to the possibility that the duty to carry out continuous assessement of abilities newly sanctioned steals time that could be better spent on improving those abilities. A plausible vision of the New Order is of teachers scurrying around their classrooms assessing, with no time to help their pupils make progress.

GCSE is still to be welcomed, for its emphasis on experience, activity, and talk—which may make Nomanslanders more prominent, and their evasions of the new tasks less easy to accommodate.

But the danger is that without improvement in certain conditions— and the next part of this book addresses this issue—the new tasks will not be asked fully of all. Nomanslanders may be subtly relegated to fetching and carrying in active parts of science lessons; to copying notes for the work of a group tackling problems in history; letting others take the lead in small group discussions. What is to act against their learned reticence? What is to prevent teachers' subtle partiality for the communicative, the active, those struggling to break through? And though the New Order dethrones stuffing, what is to prevent its subtle restoration as the proper activity for the apparently dull?

Those I saw abandoned to second-best teaching might expect rescue under the New Order; but without critical changes in conditions, erosion of certain constraints, the New Order may be subtly adjusted so that many can be relegated as effectively as before, with the evasive learning new tactics to neutralize the heady new initiatives, and dodge intrusive new demands.

Nor may the New Order press teachers to judge pupils more subtly and less glibly. The 'profile' system, for instance, asks for *more* judgements of pupils, not necessarily *better* ones. *A 'profile' of a Nomanslander might just particularize misapprehension.*

And what better aid to relegation could there be than the coming attainment tests?

PART THREE

Circumstances—constraints—
what needs to change.

CHAPTER NINE

Good circumstances: Annette's dilemma

I TOOK time off from my part-time job, and from writing this book, to teach on a short course run by a friend of mine, offering advanced foreign students of English lessons in English literature, and the chance to do all manner of other things, such as acting in short plays. I enjoy this course greatly—because I like teaching literature to foreign students, and directing plays. The work is teaching at its best, in circumstances that conspire to make it a pleasure. And I particularly liked the group I was given—teaching them for an hour and a half every day, their company a holiday from the isolation of writing.

Early on, I felt that one of them—Annette—did not think much of herself; and my interest was stirred by the possibility that she'd had the sort of education with which this book is most concerned. Something studious about her appealed to me, too. I liked the way she put on her reading glasses, and looked intently, with great concentration, at whatever text I put in front of her.

Her comments impressed me; and the clear, considered—yet sometimes hesitant—way she made them suggested the sort of ambiguity I find so interesting. She seemed shy, but sure of many of her thoughts; without much confidence, yet able when moved or interested to push doubt bravely aside in order to speak.

She seemed an ambiguous mixture of diffidence and strength; of uncertainty and conviction. Other people liked her, and were interested by her; and yet I sensed that she doubted her power to interest and attract.

Adam and Eve

Annette had elected to take part in a play. At the auditions we hold at the beginning of the course, she had not managed to act the piece she had prepared. It wasn't clear at that stage why not. She fumbled, said rather shyly that she couldn't remember the words, and left the stage in a certain amount of confusion.

To find out what her voice could be like, I had auditioned her on her own the following day—before I had got to know her at all. She spoke clearly. It was obvious she could be a competent actress. Someone needed an Eve for a pantomimic version of a mystery play; so I suggested Annette.

Meanwhile I enjoyed her contributions to my classes—as I enjoyed those of all in the group, from fastidious Jerome, to exuberant Chloe.

For the first ten days or so of rehearsals I didn't know how Annette was getting on with her play. Then, with four days to go before the performance, I watched a rehearsal of her play in the garden.

She was playing to a small audience for the first time, and she went to pieces. She seemed to have lost her voice. She looked at the ground. She moved awkwardly, as if embarrassed. She was obviously miserable.

I felt responsible, having cast her in the play in the first place. Her dilemma was acute: the others were acting freely, and she was the only one who did not seem able to produce the light, pantomimic touch. When I talked to her afterwards, she kept saying I must find another Eve, she wasn't going to manage—she would spoil it, she'd be useless. She would never be able to perform in front of other people. Her voice had gone, and would get worse.

To begin with, I just felt sorry for her and didn't know what to do. I took her through some of her words, in a room away from everyone else. But on that first occasion she seemed bowed down with a sense of having failed, and the impossibility of doing any better. We made no progress, and I felt embarrassed and constrained. I could sense that she was enduring a small, but none the less painful, crisis of confidence; and all over so trivial an affair—this footling play, designed to be fun for those taking part. Instead, for her, it seemed to be turning the last few days of the course into an ordeal.

I realized that to try to restore her acting confidence would be to return to my chosen territory—the territory of this book. I decided to do my best to offer her a different idea of what she could do in her play.

We met next day, and talked for a while about confidence. She talked of her experience as an athlete: she'd been a national champion hurdler for her age. She talked of the pressure on her to succeed, her terror of the big races, the anxiety she felt before exams. She talked of her French exam for the baccalaureate, when, she said, she'd had so many good ideas, which she then decided weren't good after all, so did not include. When she told her teacher about these ideas, he was furious and said they were wonderful. I asked her what sort of grade she'd achieved. Oh, average, she said. She talked too of a moment in one of my classes when she had wanted to make a particular point, but had not. Then, straightaway, someone else had made it, and she had kicked herself.

She was someone hovering between doubt and faith, between optimistic and pessimistic theories of her own worth and ability.

I taught her some tricks. Whether or not they helped her to perform her play, I do not know. It is possible that she would have managed perfectly all right without my coaching: performance itself often makes inexperienced and frightened actors—she had never acted before—rise to the occasion and defeat their nerves.

I taught her to stand as if she possessed the space she stood on. I tried to make her feel in command, in control, by keeping her shoulders well back, by moving more deliberately, and by always looking up. I persuaded her to tie her hair back with a handkerchief so that she could not hide, could not duck for cover behind her black curtains.

What I was doing was trying to equip her with gestures with which she could express a feeling of importance. The ruse is that by assembling the gestures appropriate to that feeling, you discover that you do, after all, possess it. You act pride, and discover that pride has been in you all the time. To use my own terminology, you experiment with a bolder theory of your own importance, only to find that part of you has believed in that theory all along. Assertion training is based on this process.

At one point in the play, for instance, Annette had been told that she must gesture behind her at—as far as I recall—the Tree of Knowledge. At first, her gesture was a constrained flutter of her hand, followed by a quick, uneasy look over her shoulder. She looked as if she were doing something which she had been told to do, but did not like doing at all. So I told her to make a simpler, larger gesture. She did so, slowly and deliberately as I wanted, and her gesture, as I told her, looked fine. Then I suggested that she should not look behind her, but should retain her command of the stage by looking ahead, fixing her gaze above the audience.

The whole sequence was transformed. She now looked authoritative, doing something she had chosen to do, showing the audience something they needed to see. She had been well directed; and she had learnt all her words and moves. What I had to do was give her the feeling—in her shoulders, in her eyes, in her voice, and in her hands—that what she was saying was important, and what she was doing needed to be seen.

I spent time on her voice. I would go as far away as possible, telling her to project to me. I felt that each time she managed to speak a line loudly and clearly, she was edging away from doubt and towards the tentative idea that she might be an actress after all.

Other people helped. She had two chances to act parts of the play in front of others before the dress rehearsal; and on both occasions she was told how well she had acted.

On the morning of the day of the performance, I produced a green handkerchief for her to try as a headband. She looked at herself wearing it, in the mirror in my classroom—and made a loud noise of disgust and horror. But what amused me was a ritual quality in her disgust at her appearance, as if part of her did realize that her uncurtained face was attractive, but couldn't quite admit it.

Her feelings about her appearance were ambiguous, expressing her conflicting ideas of her worth.

I had the same sense of her other self: positive, confident, proud, pleased with her good looks, when she came out of the make-up room that evening and into a throng of people of both sexes—who received her like royalty, making appreciative noises. A French boy, with frank admiration, said she looked great. Looking in the mirror just after her make-up had gone on, she'd said scornfully that she looked just like a doll; but now her pleasure was palpable.

And she did succeed, producing a convincing, clear, definite, funny performance. She'd been directed to play Eve as a sulky, strong-willed *ingénue*—and she'd found the confidence to do so, with additional flourishes I'd never seen before.

Her success moved me: a success which sprang from her courage to do something which she would far rather have avoided. She had experimented with the idea that she could act—against her suspicion that she could not—and her experiment had succeeded.

The parable of Annette

Annette's story is an example of the optimistic power that accompanies acknowledgement; and I would like it to be read as a parable to illumine what has most concerned me in this book.

Take, first, her small failure in that first public rehearsal as representative of all the small failures pupils and students experience in their education. There are telling similarities between her predicament then and the predicament of all who find themselves in classrooms. An audience defeated her. If I am right, and talk is crucial to learning, then each pupil's first and most awesome battle is to be able to talk in front of a large audience. Many pupils lose that battle again and again. Each defeat is a small negative resolution of ambiguity: each defeat is experimental evidence to support negative ideas of themselves.

What Annette needed, to learn that she was an actress, was for someone to acknowledge her and prove that she could indeed act, by contriving in rehearsal a series of small successes, a sequence of good experiences that gave her evidence of her competence.

But in large classes in large schools, teachers all too often cannot even sense their pupils' ambiguity; let alone identify their small defeats, or contrive the series of small victories that might lead them to accept an optimistic theory of a particular ability; and thereby—perhaps—try out a bolder notion of their own worth.

I could have accepted that Annette was not an actress, was too shy to cope with an audience—and could have pleaded on her behalf for her to leave the cast. The constraints against which teachers in schools have to work force them again and again to accept small similar defeats. But I was luckier. I was assisted by the luxurious circumstances of the course. I had time to wander up to her rehearsal, and watch it reflectively, with no need to rush off to some more urgent appointment. I had time to glimpse her individuality—being able to single her out of a small group of twelve agreeable people. But teachers in schools, always between urgencies, cannot single out each of the hundreds of pupils for whom they are responsible each week.

I needed above all to feel buoyant and contented, as I always do when teaching on that course. It was my contentment that left room in my mind for thought and curiosity. But teachers in schools often go too short of enjoyment, are hard put to feel sufficiently relaxed to think.

Annette's story is a parable about the ambiguity of adolescence—when we do not yet know anything for certain; when our ideas of ourselves and of the world are inchoate; but when institutions and authorities all too often take our ideas for finished and final.

Ambiguity continues after adolescence; but perhaps to be adult is to cope with ambiguity, admitting that the world and yourself will never be quite comprehensible. In adolescence much of our energy is devoted to the making of choices that often do seem rigid and decisive, because of our fear of uncertainty and our desire to end it. Such decisions may seem definite and finished; when truly they are no more than urgent— sometimes desperate—experiment.

Each 'decision' may be experiment to test a theory; but adults will all too often mistake experiment for incontrovertible choice. Each experiment is an attempt to resolve ambiguity; but adults too often see only the brave harshness of the attempt, mistake it for irreversible, and forget the uncertainty to which it is a response.

Adolescents frighten adults. They threaten us with their bravery, their refusal to compromise, the extremism of some of their experiment. They often show a sort of nobility, a keen sense of honour, that can belittle us. Even the beauty that some of them possess so nonchalantly can alarm us.

One way we can cope is by assuming that the adolescents we work with have made landfall in adulthood before they really have, fostering their experiments as 'good decisions' when it suits us. When we accept such 'decisions', we often make mistakes that are far more truly decisive in their effect than we begin to realize.

Suppose I had accepted Annette's 'decision' that she 'could not cope' as good enough evidence that she had quite rightly understood—being too 'shy' and 'insecure'—that she was not an actress, and 'quite unsuited to the part or to acting of any sort'. Suppose I had agreed that she should not continue: I would have prevented her from the alternative decision she subsequently made, to try to succeed, not to give in. I would have demeaned her, belittled her, accepted a diminished version of her rather than her possible self.

Finally, to continue to read this parable, take Annette's unmistakable ability as an actress—unmistakable in the end, that is—to stand for any and all of the abilities people bring with them to their education, and all abilities half disclosed, or pretending not to exist at all.

If, urgently and hurriedly, as one does in schools, I had taken what Annette showed of her acting ability in the garden as sufficient evidence on which to judge that ability, I would have relegated her to an honourable, far from ignominious category: *not an actress*. But in so doing, I would have helped to bury a talent. I would also have accepted a small defeat, and contributed to a larger sense of failure.

Schools are all too good at burying talents and confirming failure. Never deliberately; but there are just too many pupils for these things not to happen; and far too little time for the sort of reflection that would allow teachers to understand the implications of what they do, and of what they don't.

Numbers of pupils and time to think form the subject of the next part of this book.

CHAPTER TEN

Class size and stress

TEACHERS will not be free to work wisely and effectively with *most* rather than *some* of their pupils, until class size is reduced, or until much more teaching is of smaller groups than are usual at present.

The comprehensive system attempts to offer equality of opportunity. But teachers will not be able to realize this aim until the problem of class size is addressed. All they can do at present is to divide their unwieldy crowds into those they can teach and like, those they can leave to get on with it, and those whose capacity to make their lives difficult they can suffer, suppress, outwit, or try to ignore.

Schools should be able to engage the evasive, as well as celebrate those well equipped by background or disposition to gain from their education. They should be able to offer a powerful challenge to influences in some pupils' lives that militate against education.

To acquire such power, schools need to be staffed by teachers able to make relationships with most of their pupils. More important, teachers need to be able to *see* their pupils clearly, in the same way that I was able to see Annette.

Large classes make visibility a privilege, not a right. It is the fate of those in Nomansland that most vividly illustrates this fact. At the Ashby Unit, we had enough staff, enough time to think, enough freedom from stress, and enough energy and enthusiasm to see our patients clearly and offer them opportunity to change. But to qualify to come to us, adolescents had to be psychiatrically ill. With more intelligent use of number, and with more time for teachers to think about their pupils and discuss them with each other, schools could be as powerful and effective as we were often able to be for our privileged patients.

A comparison of teaching small and large classes

Feelings

The key advantage of small classes is not so much that there is more time for each pupil—though that is a huge benefit—but that the quality of the teacher's attention will be higher, because, like his pupils, he will be more likely to feel relaxed. Those pupils likely to find large numbers intimidating feel safer when numbers are smaller. The effect of smaller numbers on a teacher is to generate the same feeling of greater safety. It is difficult to be spontaneous, generous, perceptive, authoritative, as one teacher responsible for twenty-five pupils. With fifteen, these things begin to become possible. To put the issue at its most basic: the larger the number of pupils, the greater a teacher's defensiveness and anxiety; the smaller, the greater the possibility of feeling relaxed, and of feeling 'parental' towards more than a minority of any class. If a teacher feels relaxed and contented, she is more likely to feel open, and ready to take risks; to be capable of affection, laughter and excitement, and generous revision of earlier opinions about her pupils.

A relaxed teacher is less likely to put up with fatuous stuffing, private passivity, learning by rote, and exercises from the book. She will be more likely to want her pupils to talk, to take risks, to discuss; to be adventurous; to take initiatives; to learn what it is to be responsible for yourself and attentive to the needs of others.

By large class, I mean over fifteen; and, as any group of teachers will tell you, classes of fifteen are far less common than classes of twenty-five. Figures for pupil : teacher ratios confuse this matter. To calculate these, the number of teachers in a school or an area is expressed in proportion to the number of children being taught. But teachers are included in the arithmetic who teach half a timetable, or a quarter, or not at all.

That an overall ratio in one particular school might be one to seventeen, is perfectly consistent with the fact that in the school concerned a typical teacher will spend her day like this:

Period 1   1st Year   28
     2   3rd Year   26
     3   5th Year   22
          BREAK
     4   6th Year   11 (Remember: most teachers do not
                          teach 6th forms)
     5   Free
          LUNCH (Marshalling a crowd of hundreds, when on duty)
     6   2nd Year   30
     7 }
     8 } 4th Year   27

What does it feel like, spending day after day dealing with such numbers? In this teacher's week, there will be days when her timetable is far more dominated by her largest classes: when, for instance, she might have her 1st Year class for a double lesson, followed by her 4th Year for another double; and after lunch spend another double lesson with her 2nd Year.

A good idea would be to test your own feelings whenever you are in a full bus, or among any large group of people. Forget that you are one of them, and imagine that you are their manager, sister, brother, parent, encyclopaedia and sergeant-major. Imagine also that among them are adolescents whose habit is to savage adults, directly or subtly. You have to outwit them for the sake of the others. Imagine, too, that you have to find some reward—so you will try to find some friends among the throng, and make them like you, and do your best for them.

It is in part sheer number that forces teachers to form small families of acknowledged pupils—in order to survive psychologically, outnumbered in a crowd; in order to protect themselves. Those pupils the interviewed teachers said they liked—the vocal ones, the strugglers, the ones who get there in the end—are loyal cohorts of kin, who stand around their besieged teachers in phalanxes of warmth and respect and pleasure.

Even in so short a time as three weeks, Annette's group of twelve began to feel united; to feel like a sort of family. In so saying, I do not mean to sound sentimental; but how else to describe the pleasure all often seemed to have in each other's company; the sense that hostility was manageable, useful; that differences of opinion would be fertile rather than fatal? The members of the group were older than school pupils; but I have had the same experience on the rare occasions when I have been able to teach adolescents in so small a group.

In a crowd of twenty-five or more, all is usually different. Subgroups form, sometimes hostile and opposed, or walled by silence in protective isolation; and a teacher has to be referee between them, minimizing enmity.

In a group of fifteen or twelve, a teacher can become truly *in loco parentis*, able to acknowledge most or even all of her pupils. A class of fifteen or twelve *feels* different from one of twenty-five in such a way that a teacher of the smaller number is less concerned with control, less preoccupied with the need for order. Twenty-five or more people forced to sit in a room are daunting; fifteen are far less so.

Preoccupation with control is greater with a larger number, because of the greater probability of split, faction, scapegoats, playing to an audience—every large class produces its clown or clowns. The greater insecurity of being responsible for a large number makes a teacher worry about control; and many pupils react to a similar sense of insecurity by withdrawing into passivity, opting for disengagement and alienation. In a small group, there is less need for the cautious— for whatever reason—to skulk, dissemble, camouflage themselves; to waste their intelligence on psychological survival in circumstances that frighten them.

With twenty-five or more to manage, a teacher can be forced, by her anxiety to control, to distance herself from many in the class, and from the class as a whole. The more threatening a class, the more likely a teacher is to remain at the front of the room, watchful and bossy. But with fifteen and under, the potential threat of disorder is so much less that a teacher can risk the proximity without which acknow-ledgement cannot exist; without which many pupils cannot become visible.

Safety relaxes; fear tightens, sends up barriers, forces people into hid-ing. It is large numbers that create the need for camouflage.

Important for my concern with the abashed and withdrawn is that a teacher of fifteen or less can feel sufficiently safe to provoke—kindly— her more elusive pupils, in attempts to encourage their participation. But provocation of any sort, however benignly intended, with a class of twenty-five or more, can run counter to the urgent need to keep the peace.

Learning

Perhaps the most important advantage of smaller numbers is that a small group can be a safe setting for the articulation of half-formed, hesitant thoughts; the necessity of which Douglas Barnes has tellingly argued.

All thinking depends on the achievement of clarity—on stages of muddle, confusion and hesitant elaboration. An empowered teacher, able to enlist the co-operation, patience and generosity of pupils in a small group, can guarantee time for hesitation. In large classes, hesitant elaboration of a thought halts momentum, can provoke scorn from the impatient. It is difficult in a large class—unless of very biddable pupils—to let any sort of pause in discussion last for very long. Discipline needs briskness and momentum. In a group of twelve or fifteen, the impatient are more easily restrained.

More crucially, if discussion—with a smaller number—were to become the central, rather than a peripheral, mode of learning, the necessity for hesitation would soon be understood by all—because all would have the opportunity to learn that thinking aloud is enjoyable. I suspect, too, that there is more likelihood in the smaller group for the donning and doffing of different roles. M. J. Abercrombie, in her book, *The Anatomy of Judgement*, shows how, in a series of sessions of discussion-learning with a group of twelve medical students, different sorts of demeanour were regularly exchanged. The impatient and vociferous learnt the value of listening and tackling questions less urgently; and those who had at first seemed 'natural' listeners became in some sessions active contributors.

I have found that there is a tendency for learning in a smaller group to revert to discussion. Discussion seems to be the natural state of learning in a group of about twelve. Lecturing, hectoring, acting, bemoaning seem all too often to attend learning in crowds of twenty-five or more; or formalized question-and-answer sessions, such as the French lessons I observed in the middle school, when so many were excluded.

With fifteen or less in a class, when someone asks a question or prompts discussion, a skilled tactician can lead all or most to profitable participation. But with twenty-five or more, a question and its consequent ripples of discussion can often be threatening (and the ripples will not reach all), because one question from the member of a certain faction will often provoke the member of another faction to throw a large irrelevance into a far corner of the debate, and soak everyone. The unpredictability of what may ensue from an unprompted question is often far harder to bear with a large number than with a small. Unpredictability is vital for active learning; but seldom welcome to teachers of large classes.

Unprompted questions and free discussion—two very important elements of learning—are often deliberately avoided by teachers of large classes. In a small group, hostile reception by X of Y's comment is more likely to be welcomed for its potential to provoke thought. In a class of twenty-five, any hostility may be dangerous.

As a result of their fear of the unpredictable, many teachers of large classes in comprehensive schools develop a pacific, appeasing style that has nothing to do with good learning, but everything to do with the outwitting of anarchy.

Earlier in this section, it was suggested that to understand what large classes feel like, feelings in kindred circumstances are useful. Perhaps the best way of describing what twelve or less feels like in comparison to a much larger number is this: the smaller number is psychologically akin to a number of familiar and agreeable circumstances: a meal with a large group of friends and family; a group of people sitting around two tables in a pub; two families spending the day together. But twenty-five or more, or even twenty? What situation in ordinary life is comfortable kin to being responsible for such a number of people younger than yourself?

For me, when I began teaching, the only kindred situation was acting to an audience, which is why I became a histrionic sort of pedagogue, feeding lines to my 'plants'.

In loco parentis: *the teacher's authority in small groups*

The committee

Smaller numbers empower and enhance teachers; greater numbers diminish and deplete them.

Two years ago, teaching a similar group to Annette's, on the same course, I set them to work on a 'simulation'. A disparate group of twelve European sixth-formers and undergraduates had to turn themselves into a committee formed by a village to discuss a proposal to build a community centre. Each student was allocated a role; each role was distinct and active, from a shopkeeper with three children who wanted somewhere for them to play sport in the evenings, to a misanthropic antique dealer who hated all noise and all youth.

I had not long been researching for this book; and I can still recall my fascination when—in role, using the logic of their positions—two students provoked another two, patiently and kindly, to make contributions. The provoked had until then been overawed by the more vocal. My attempts to winkle them out had not been particularly successful in other sessions. But lured out of their disengagement by their peers, they came to life. One, in the role of a mother of young twins, became as active as any of the more 'naturally' vocal. She took from the experience the pleasure of trying out another self, like new clothes she hadn't dared to think she could buy. She had been wanting to jump out of silence and into talk. It had been my job to contrive circumstances that allowed her to do so; and afterwards to confirm her success, to acknowledge and underwrite it, awarding her plenty of opportunity to continue to participate.

If a group is small, a teacher can frequently contrive such moments. A teacher of twelve or fifteen can harness the group's energy, exploit its generosity.

The boy who felt words as bullets

I recall a boy at the Ashby Unit who was so withdrawn, and so frightened of other people, that when you passed him in a corridor he would flinch; if you spoke to him he would look at you as if you had punched him; when you looked into his face, he would duck away as if your eyes were hot. He managed to confess once that words said to him felt like bullets fired at him.

The traitor phantasy he had to defeat was that people did not want *him* to talk to *them*; that people were scornful, hostile and contemptuous; that he was unworthy of attention. In social skills training sessions, we tried to contrive experience for him which might suggest that he was not after all the contemptible creature he felt others would see if he tried to make contact with them.

I recall a group of nine other patients forming a queue at a bus stop. Peter's task was to ask one of them the time. His phantasy—his hypothesis—told him that to do so was to earn derision.

We persuaded him to try. We primed him to ask three patients, in a certain order. We primed the first two not to know. Gangly and hesitant, he asked each in turn the time, being told in the end what it was. We asked the three what it had felt like to be asked. Nothing special, they said. We asked Peter what it felt like to ask.

'Terrible', he said.

'But they didn't think it was terrible, did they?' we told him.

We played the scene back on the television. We asked everyone what they thought of his manner. All agreed it was 'okay', 'nothing special'. There was a feeling that he had been a bit hesitant.

We tried it again, asking him to try to be a bit more forceful. Already buoyed up by the evidence he had been shown that people did not find him ludicrous and contemptible, he looked less gangly and awkward, and spoke more clearly. This time, when we watched his attempt on the screen, there was a fusion of respect and appreciation: he was far better, all agreed.

He was now more than pleased: he was excited. He was sensing his freedom to be another person—a freedom offered by his peers' spontaneous responses, by his courage, and by our parental manipulations. His traitor phantasy—his traitor hypothesis—had been exposed, sentenced, and executed.

Such an episode is a model for the sort of work that could lead an evasive or over-cautious member of a small group of twelve to participate in discussion, rather then opt out. But such work would be far more difficult, and probably impossible, with a crowd—just as group psychotherapy will not succeed if a certain critical number is exceeded.

A simulation such as my village committee cannot be done with a crowd. Discussion can be carried off by a good authoritative teacher with a crowd of twenty-five; but twelve or so pupils will be the chief contributors—while, with a difficult class, the exhibitionistic hostility of six others is kept at bay, the silence of five pupils is ignored, the misery of one other not even seen, and the uncontrollable diversions of the class clown are as tactfully as possible outmanœuvred.

Splitting crowds into groups

It is possible to split crowds into groups for the specific purpose of discussion and collaborative learning—such as I saw in the English lesson in the middle school. But it is only with relatively peaceable pupils that this tactic is effective; and with any sort of pupils, it is difficult to manage well.

The feeling of being in a crowd is not easily dismissed by this tactic: it is impossible to forget the presence of other groups from your position as a member of one of them—if only because of the noise they make. And for a teacher, twenty-eight is still twenty-eight, whether in four groups of seven or as one bloc of twenty-eight.

The feeling of being in a crowd works actively against the creation in each group of the family coherence necessary for collaboration and discussion. Currents of hostility between groups are ruinous. The hesitant may feel no safer then when in rows facing the front.

A teacher, dodging from group to group, quelling hostility, explaining material, trying to assess the quality of a discussion here, answering a question there—cannot be the facilitator that good group work needs. Using groups will lead to more participation, more active learning, than if groups are not used. But the quality of the work achieved in such groups—especially with pupils older and more potentially wayward then those I watched in the English lesson—will be nothing like as high as that achievable by a teacher working with a single group of twelve; or facilitating the work of three groups of five in a class of fifteen.

Teachers often give up the group work they are told to contrive when they are trained, because they know, without having time to think it out and understand why not, that they cannot.give groups the conditions they need to work successfully.

The difficulties of keeping order can be great. Discussion creates noise. How is a teacher, talking to one group, to tell good noise from bad noise in the group two away from her at the far end of the room? Imagine, too, what it feels like, if discussion is going well in all five groups of six in a crowd of thirty. How much productive excitement can a teacher bear before the sheer volume of noise becomes intolerable?

In drama classes I would always divide a crowd—say—of thirty into five groups of six. I would set them improvisations to do. Loving the work, the vociferous in each group would get carried away. Soon the noise would reach the level at which I would fear visits from irate neighbours of the Old School; and my own tolerance would be wearing thin. Time and again, I would end improvisations too soon. Time and again, I would feel reluctant to let them begin, especially if I were feeling tired and stressed half-way through the afternoon.

Large classes have their deleterious effect on teachers' competence chiefly because of the stress they cause. I have touched on several other disadvantages of large number; but stress is the gravest of all of them; and their inevitable concomitant. Stress can be of two kinds.

'Good' stress

Imagine that the teacher whose day I timetabled was me in 1975, teaching in Glentoul. Join me, waiting last lesson in the afternoon for a crowd of thirty-two 13-year-olds to come down to the assembly hall—where all my drama lessons take place.

All day, in varying degrees, they have been enduring some of the frustration I watched in the middle school. But drama is a release from all that. They want to shout, run, make ludicrous faces, mime obscenities. They want to purge themselves of boredom and patience. They want to have a good time.

Six crowds have come into, and then left, my room before I face the onslaught of emotion I have now to endure. In each crowd there was a bewildering mixture of attitudes and dispositions. Each fizzed with hilarity; but was also sodden with sadness. Each had a clown or two, some scapegoats, a tyrant. Each had its Nomansland—though I did not know it. Each had its share of pupils whose relations with their parents were so explosive that any adult working with them could become a target for their projections, their attempts to resolve confusion. And each crowd was possible chaos that had to be dominated. Dominion is exhausting.

The first two pupils I notice as the crowd comes in are the two most difficult. I notice them before any of the others, already vigilant for the trouble they might cause. They are far more prominent in class than any of the others—except for four very gifted pupils, wonderful actors, whom it is my pleasure to watch.

The first of these 'difficult' pupils is a girl: precociously developed, volatile, imaginative, intelligent—and often unhappy. I can sense straight away that some probably small event has triggered this unhappiness. She enters in full sulk, and I then have a complex mixture of feelings: commiseration, because I like her; irritation, because I am tired and because her explosions when they come can be powerful; and amusement, at her miniature-Bardot, pouting discontent.

The other 'problem' is nicknamed 'pissy Paul'. He has a bladder complaint that makes him smell slightly of urine all the time. He too is unhappy. He is always unhappy; but today more than usually so. No doubt, in the chaos of the lesson they have just had—with a teacher who is not at all good at keeping order—his taunters had freedom to heap misery on his head.

A measure of the stress of dealing with this crowd is that my imagination refuses to produce any sympathy for Paul. I cannot cope with the thought of him. His misery is too extreme. I have no space or time to encompass it. I shelve him; but make myself vigilant for trouble that may erupt around him.

The rest? A baffling hotch-potch of biography; various human beings for now all seeming the same: prisoners escaping from gaol. School does that: it is not just clothes that are required to be uniform. Postures and voices and the expressions on faces are prone to spells of apparent uniformity that help to mislead teachers into generalization.

I summon my dwindling stock of energy and begin. First, order has to be established. Noise is stressful: it makes me feel as if I were about to be overwhelmed. There is stress, too, in my ambivalence about noise: the Dionysian part of me welcomes it, knows that drama needs misrule in order to be successful. But I am also very tired, and very conscious of the coming and going of dominies of the Old School, some of whom disapprove of drama, and disapprove of it most of all when I give misrule some rope, and the children make a NOISE.

I think that the same ambivalence exists, and is a cause of stress, in all lessons in all subjects with large classes. Teachers want their pupils to be active, to enjoy learning, to be energetic. They want the sort of learning of which I saw so little in the middle school, and which is much easier to organize in a small group. They often want some noise as evidence of energy and enjoyment. But anxiety about disorder is in opposition to this healthy desire. So teachers are torn: and stress is the result. I have watched lessons when you could see these two conflicting forces—desire for energy; fear of disorder—tearing a teacher's peace of mind apart. It does not surprise me that the fear of disorder can be so great that it forces teachers to satisfy their desire for active learning covertly, with their kin, the members of their 'families'.

I establish order with a shout. The chairs are cleared away to make a big space. While this is being done, Paul throws a big punch at one of his tormentors, and I have to soothe him, sit him down out of trouble, and tell the tormentor to see me after the lesson. I have no idea what I will say to him.

The exercises begin, for all except Paul. I am conscious of him all the time, despite my attempts to shelve the thought of him. I try to force myself not to attend to the sadness he makes me feel.

I love watching the exercises because the children enjoy them so fully, so uncompromisingly. For the first, I ask them to walk in a variety of ways: as if on ice, and barefoot; in thick, wet mud; against a high wind; dodging thrown stones. I call the changes like a dancing master. They shriek, whoop, shout. The noise is legitimate; but it has an extra force to it which is the result of the day-long storing of frustration. That force, despite my pleasure and my intention that they should enjoy themselves freely, is frightening. Think of thirty-one people screaming; thirty-one people at the back of whose minds there lurks a phantasy of the destruction of all schools.

As this exercise progresses, the part of me that longs for peace and order, and knows so well that children need structure, need boundaries, gains ascendancy.

'On scorpions!' I shout, in one last bid for misrule; and then, 'Freeze!'—the ritual order for silence and immobility. The postures they hold entrance me. The room has filled with statuary, expressive of a vast range of different emotions and intentions.

In each of the subsequent exercises—improvisations, mime, games for voice—the force of stored frustration is still there, and still frightening. It is not that anarchy may break out at any moment; but that it feels as if it may. What causes stress is that, although I am an effective manager of the lesson, sheer number and the force of the pupils' feelings make me *feel* incompetent. I feel up against it; I feel that I must be failing—because I am so heavily outnumbered, and responsible for everything that happens.

I feel thus despite the fact that the children are obviously enjoying themselves; that in improvisations they are talking more freely and to greater purpose than they probably have all day; that in everything they do their knowledge of people and their imaginations are being put to use. I know that I am being successful; but I feel overwhelmed, and more and more like a prison warder about to deal with a riot.

I am torn between what my mind tells me and my emotions shriek at me. Teachers are for ever thus torn, when numbers are enormous.

I am so far from being relaxed, that it makes me impercipient. I do not notice that some are not taking as active a part as they might; I do not see my Nomanslanders who need to be lured to activity and prominence. I do not count the number of people in groups established for improvisations who, allocated a role, do nothing with it, but find passivity and wrap it round themselves.

My hidden fear makes me feel, quite erroneously, that *all* may soon riot. Pupils phantasize about the destruction of schools; teachers' equivalent phantasy is of riot.

The chief source of stress, then, is a phantasy that makes me afraid. Its chief results are fatigue, impercipience, and anxiety; a defensiveness against the prospect of being overwhelmed; an ability to see only the crowd. But in ironic counterpoint to this tendency to see all my pupils as one unanimous danger, is a tendency to hold fast to what I feel I *do* know about *some* individuals (while ignoring many others, and claiming that I know them, when in fact I do not).

Being responsible for a crowd forces a teacher to claim and foreclose knowledge of her pupils on far too scant evidence. But there is a deeper dimension to this process. The stress of being responsible for too many, gives each claim to knowledge of an individual a defensive, protective importance. In predicaments that alarm us or make us uneasy, explanation and interpretation are reassuring. The more the stress, the greater the urgency to explain.

This means that all through the lesson I manage stress in two ways. The first is by bringing noisy exercises to an end before I should, or doing quieter ones instead. The second is by focusing my attention on the pupils I can most easily explain and understand. So I watch the stars: the brilliant mimes, the most expressive improvisers, the virtuosi. I feel safer being able to explain what's happening as I watch them: here are people who are *good at drama*. And my explanation, chosen to make me feel better, does so. My choice of who to watch is a choice of those whose explanation gives me most satisfaction and most reassurance.

When the unhappy girl screams at a boy and bursts into tears, I first receive this as a threat to my safety; but I soon explain it. The current myth about the girl concerns half-understood stories of her home life. Home is to blame, I decide. Her anarchic misery is therefore manageable, less stressful: I don't need to think about her any more. I tell her tormentor to wait until the end of the lesson to see me, rejoin her to her group, and take my attention elsewhere.

Stress makes teachers endlessly explain. Too many children and adolescents are caught in explanations that are far from accurate and further from helpful. *Stress contributes to misjudgement.*

All possible reactions

Imagine yourself in a bus again, responsible for a varied mass of people. You, like me, have a number of possible ways, or likely ways, of reacting to various emotions and different sorts of behaviour. Certain emotions arouse feelings that prompt certain reactions. By the time my drama lesson has come to an end, a very large proportion of my full range of reactions has been provoked—though not in all cases expressed; and the suppression entailed is itself a cause of further stress.

The range of emotions presented to me is enormous. In some part of my mind, at different levels of awareness, I am reacting to them all, and suppressing most of my reactions. Somewhere in my mind the misery I feel for Paul is lodged. Elsewhere there is hilarity at the exuberance of some; irritation, sensual pleasure, anger, aesthetic delight, empathy, hostility. Moving among all these feelings is fear.

My mind is overstretched, to say the least. I do not believe that the layman can have any adequate idea of the pain and the ferocity of that stretching until he has had the experience of being responsible for so large a number. My mind is under efficient management because I am experienced: I know what I am doing. I am also buoyed up by a feeling of success: I know I am doing well. What's more, I am enjoying myself. But that, oddly, does not make what I am doing any less stressful. Pleasure at my competence, at the delight of some of my pupils, *adds* to stress, because it runs counter to so many of my other feelings. It adds a new tension; pulls against fear, fatigue, and sympathetic sadness.

Stress forces relegation—forced me to relegate Paul to a region where my imagination did not easily travel, even though I could not forget him altogether. I would have liked to have been able to forget him; because in so doing I would have subtracted from the total stress of my predicament. And I did manage to relegate many of his classmates—those who made no call on my attention, and who did not appeal to my appreciation. Their presence added to the number of the crowd, and so to my fear; but by benignly neglecting them, I could lessen that fear, in a paradoxical sleight of mind by which, fearing their presence, I pretended their absence.

There were perhaps ten of these in all: the ones who took passive roles in improvisations; who got on quietly in pairs with mime exercises they could manage, but in which they could not excel; who in phases of misrule, kept control of themselves, were a little inhibited, would not let themselves go.

Paradox rules all in large-class teaching. They were enemies because they bulked the crowd; but allies because they were compliant. They were 'good' pupils; but they were not being pushed or stretched or invited to experiment. Among them was certainly a pupil who could have benefited from my attention, an Annette who felt that, whenever she took part in an improvisation, she had failed.

I did not winkle out such pupils, even had I known they were there for the winkling. They were too useful to me as they were.

The cumulative effect of such stress

The gradual effect of such stress as I have described is more impercipience, less sympathy, more fear; and—worst of all—more deep fatigue. Not a physical tiredness so much as a gradual death of interest in one's pupils; so that, after ten years' teaching, fewer and fewer tempt you to acknowledge them.

This fatigue may be encountered in most staffrooms, where can be heard the dismissive, disappointed talk that it produces. There will always be exceptions: people who have the luck to possess some inner resistance to such erosion. There are those, too, whose early skill and success take them away from classrooms and into offices for most of their time. They often remain lively, interested, perceptive and compassionate.

I left teaching in comprehensive schools in order to work in a psychiatric ward—the Ashby Unit. There, I found stress: the stress of working exclusively with the damaged, the disconsolate and the mad. But there were so many members of staff; and there was time for all of us to think and talk and help each other, so that stress could be dissipated, and our energies recharged.

Teaching large classes in schools, you go from stress to stress, with no pause to relax, think, understand, recuperate. Stress builds and builds inside you.

At the Ashby Unit, I did not know at first how to cope with the absence of the sort of stress I was used to. Just as I missed my audiences, I also—paradoxically again—missed that very stress. It can become addictive, producing regular bouts of mania; while your capacity to be thoughtful and curious is being steadily eroded. It offers pseudo-excitement—nothing whatever to do with the authentic pleasure of giving full attention to the complexity of the pupils you are teaching; while appreciating the extraordinary complexity of the process of learning itself.

I have discovered those pleasures since ceasing to work in schools.

'Bad' stress

I went back to school briefly at the beginning of last year. I took on some supply teaching at Marston—the city school where I taught after leaving Scotland. There for the first time I experienced a riot, which reminded me of a kind of stress far graver than what I have just described. Some teachers experience this second sort of stress quite regularly; and all teachers experience it early in their careers, as part of the process of their initiation.

I was to teach a third-year class social studies, last lesson on a Wednesday. Typically of the school, the teacher for whom I was covering had gone to enormous trouble to set and prepare suitable work. All I had to do was hand it out, supervise it, and collect it.

Two street scenes, photographed, with descriptions in words, were given to pupils to compare: one of the New Town in Edinburgh, the other of a familiar scene of dereliction nearer home. A tendentious exercise, perhaps; but I looked forward to a preliminary discussion of the pictures, even though I had been told they were a 'low-stream' class of 13- to 14-year-olds, and would probably be difficult.

Seriously weakened by a girl in a fifth-year class, who had destroyed the lesson before by fluent, unrestrained assault on my attempts to interest her class in a text about euthanasia—I was not in a good state for what followed.

The attack came in waves: twos and threes at first, arguing loudly; and finally, a great onslaught of the rest, twenty-seven in all. My restraining noises (had I really once been able to persuade classes to wait outside rooms?) were not noticed.

Initially they did sit down, to hear about and disapprove of the work I was to give them. Dogged, as yet refusing to shout, I handed out the papers. A tall girl 'on report' threw at me the paper on which I had to account for her behaviour during the lesson, and shouted at me not to forget to sign it. Another girl, whom, I confess, I came in thirty-five minutes to hate, had stolen and hidden this tall girl's bag. Finding it again managed to uproot at least ten others from their seats, scuffling and swearing and shouting; yelling that maniacal yell that I had not heard since last teaching at this school, six years before.

Futilely, I tried to make my own large voice compete. I willed myself to master the class. But it was impossible. A fight began between two girls. They squared up to each other like Edwardian pugilists. Their insults grew vivid and hysterical. I moved to separate them, while the rest of the class rose to applaud and exhort and incite—and yell.

A novice in separating girl fighters, I was worried about accusations of being violent myself. But another girl came to my rescue: she separated them, shoved them back in their seats, and yelled at them to shut up and stop it. Others, disgruntled, yelled at her to mind her own business. But her yell was the most potent in the room, and she won.

By then, crowd hysteria had taken over. It peaked in about five minutes, though it felt far longer. Everyone seemed to have a stake in the abandoned fight. I wondered if I dared go for help, without worse happening if I left.

In the end, a sort of temporary calm developed, but not because of anything I had done. Some set to work. A girl in the front row, who had been doing so throughout, went on asking me questions, relevant and intelligent, which I could at last hear and attend to. Noise threatened to rise again; but the bell saved me.

As riots go, I don't think it was a bad one. Another girl in the front row reminisced afterwards about a far more exciting affair, when it had taken six teachers to restore order. But it depressed me. So did the reaction of a senior member of staff when I told her what had happened. She made it quite clear that I was reporting a regular occurrence.

It has to be said that Marston is not an easy school. But the second sort of stress I have just described, extreme though my example of it may be, is not rare, and is not confined to 'difficult' inner city schools. I experienced it many times—though never so outrageously—in Glentoul.

The effect of this graver stress is to make teachers fearful; to confirm whatever anxiety their phantasies already provide. It also confirms the ambiguity of perception that teachers have of their classes: seeing them as threatening blocs of hostility, and yet differentiating them with spurious clarity into tagged individuals. He's a troublemaker; she's a nice quiet girl. A riot makes the need for such explanation not just important, but imperative.

Grave stress, and the fear of it, can force teachers behind all sorts of defences which make it difficult for them to emerge and acknowledge their pupils, or promote active co-operative learning. Take two of the most typical. The first is the defence of becoming a martinet. This entails the honing of preternatural vigilance for trouble; the pouncing on potential troublemakers before they have so much as opened their mouths. This is the defensive use of explanation as first strike. But the trouble is that the original impulse to defend—individuality, peace of mind, the ability to sleep, sanity—turns into a habit of neurotic aggression that can become hard to shift.

I have already mentioned the opposite defence: the diplomat, soother of conflict, oiler of ruffled seas. This depends on a different sort of vigilance, but one equally productive of blindness; for if you are vigilant for trouble to soothe, what room do you have in your mind for awareness of those who need your help to learn? This different vigilance is a constant tired sandpapering of all the rough edges of your minute by minute reactions to stress and provocation, and small and large irritations. I certainly used this defence after my first traumatic year at Glentoul, when I experienced plenty of the second sort of stress. It means that your attention is constantly distracted inwards, by the need to monitor and control over-reactions which you know would cause yet more trouble; and it leads from the critical early experience of the ineffectual results of shouting, and your rejection, for ideological or other reasons, of the martinet defence.

Riots do not happen easily with twelve pupils. Riots, and the hectic over-excitement that produces them, are a product of large numbers. Smaller numbers would multiply parental relationships between teachers and pupils. Pupils would not behave as my rioting class did if held tightly by the security created by adults, empowered to work as strong parents. Better, fiercer discipline isn't the answer. It is too late for that. Deference has gone, and whips wouldn't bring it back. Power and authority are the answer; but the power and authority that attend adults who are free to act strongly.

Time to think

Stress can force teachers into making their primary concern the need to survive with their sense of self intact—or nearly intact. Nothing in my teaching career has been as demoralizing as the sort of experience I have just described. It is usually in their early years that teachers are victims of similar ordeals, so that the need to survive becomes a priority at the outset of a teacher's career; or, if not a priority, then an abiding concern leading to all sorts of impercipience.

Perhaps even worse than this, an effect of such stress is to make *thought* about what you are doing, less of a pleasure, less of a necessity, to be if possible avoided. Your mind shies away from thought about the source of your worst fears and anxieties. You may become something of an automaton; and it is even more likely that your rewards will be on the black market of covert tuition of your 'family'.

All in all, it is miraculous that so many teachers in so many schools manage to retain humanity—reserving its benefits, of course, for a minority of their pupils. But many burn out too soon. Too many become disappointed and embittered. An ex-headmaster puts the point like this:

Finally I would observe that on the whole teachers are expected to undertake too many contact hours per week so that full-time classroom teaching is a young person's game. Promotion [to administrative roles that require less teaching] is essential if physical health is to be maintained as one grows older. With promotion coming less easily, some alternative is necessary, and varying one's commitment so that some part of one's time is spent as a teaching auxiliary and preferably also that some time is spent *with* small groups. [My italics.]   (R. Spooner, *Education*, no. 22, 1 June 1979, p. 636.)

Behind that flat phrase 'too many contact hours', you must imagine crowds on crowds on crowds on crowds. So many of them, coming so fast in ebullient noisy succession into your room, that your power to make sensible discriminations between pupil and pupil, to perceive individuality and complexity—dies.

An ex-pupil's solutions

I now want to turn to the suggestions made by a boy I met and interviewed at David's FE college.

Mark was one of the most interesting people I talked to. When I met him, he was a follower of the New Romantic fashion. He looked Byronic, with wide black breeches and a flounced white shirt. He was good-looking and tall, and in a sea of denim, in his flamboyant dress he seemed to be challenging himself to be singular. He was taking A levels, after leaving school with seven O levels, some of them A's. But far from feeling himself to have been an academic success, he was disenchanted, cynical about schools and education, and very, very tired. I felt he might not put very much into his A level studies.

What he says adds up to a statement whose implication is clear: Mark found the experience of being in school an assault on what he felt himself to be. His response to not being acknowledged was not to evade and disappear, but the opposite: to be strident, wilful, difficult. I suspect that his teachers found someone so strong and so intelligent extremely threatening.

Talking of a day when he felt bloody-minded, and full of scorn for the futility of what he was being asked to do so much of the time, he says that a teacher, seeing him not doing anything, said:

Do your work! And I said that I just couldn't be bothered to do it. Right, he said, down to the headmaster, how dare you say a thing like that in my class . . .

A less daunting and inflammatory pupil would have been easily out-manoeuvred after saying such a thing.

Mark experienced a feeling of alienation; but he reacted aggressively rather than passively.

It's totally anti-human, in a way, anti-personal. Everyone's conscious that they are pupils or that they are teachers. I don't think I ever managed to talk to the people there as adults or as human beings.

There was one exception, a history teacher, of whom he says, interestingly:

He was a good teacher, and he was a good bloke. He had more in common with the people he was teaching—he made jokes about things that other teachers might have found a bit embarrassing. He wasn't weak, he was strong, he let us have a bit of leeway.

This strength I take to be the expression of a relaxed and acceptable authority; from someone strong enough to feel a minimum of anxiety, so that he can allow 'leeway' without sacrificing order; someone confident enough to allow a certain degree of proximity to his pupils; able to use the power that a confident parent can use.

But of most of his time at school, Mark says:

I don't think ordinary relationships come into the education of an ordinary person for the whole of the eleven years they're there. I don't think they're allowed to be a person, allowed to have emotions, allowed to say, God, I didn't do my work today because I felt down about it.

I then said: 'It's odd, because that phase of secondary school life—' But Mark cut me short, knowing what I was talking about.

—is when you're growing and you're grasping and you're trying to under-stand . . . and you're actually developing from a little blob of flesh that was breast-fed and spoon-fed to something that should be able to feed itself, but they still manage to do the spoon-feeding all the way through.

His savage comments about his teachers suggest strongly that he feels that ordinary relationships, ordinary behaviour, are impossible in school. He depicts, in caricature, teachers forced into ludicrous posturing; forced by stress, by the erosion of their generosity and peace of mind by the succession of crowds passing through their rooms:

The whole system was totally stupid. Some teachers I thought were just total idiots, I don't think they deserved any respect whatsoever. They way they portrayed themselves—I found them for the most part, you know, boorish, egotistical, self-worshipping. So petty: they were the demigods, they were in the position of power, and these silly little kids were all getting under their feet.

He dealt with school by acting up, by being difficult, by being what he says his teachers called 'immature':

Coming here [to the FE college] was a great escape from all that . . . The thing is, did I behave stupidly because they treated me like that, or was it the other way round? But here I'm the same person, I still make jokes and things, but they don't turn round and ask you to repeat what you've said, and that kind of thing.

I got really paranoid about not being able to be myself. My way of behaving was just a kind of defence, a way of surviving.

I got four A's, two B's and a C for O level. I got an A for English, for the guy I hated, which just showed him. I think I really shocked everyone, my final two fingers up to them; and leaving, showing they'd got me all wrong.

They had kept telling him that unless he changed his 'attitude', he would fail.

In our second interview, I asked Mark what he thought might change all this. First we talked over the possibility that school exists to 'social-ize' children; that its chief purpose is to set boundaries to individuality, and train for a life of compromise. But I think we both shared, without making it explicit, a belief that schools could and should be better places, where individuals could be encouraged to think for themselves.

He pointed to one great fault in schools as he had known them:

At the moment there's the very deep gap between the teacher and the pupil: the teachers at one end and the pupils at the other behind their desks; and there's a tremendous gap between adult and child.

And the solution he proposed was:

Get rid of the complete and utter gap. I think one way to do it would be to have smaller classes, so that you can actually relate to each other as people, as human beings.

At the moment the discipline's got to be maintained: that is why the teachers have got to keep themselves apart, to maintain these barriers, to make the system function. Perhaps if you could remove those distances, you could let them see each other as people.

Here he makes my point about the need for control forcing teachers to keep their distance from their pupils.

He suggested that on his side of the gap, deception and disguise—the equivalents of the evasions that have played a large part in this book—were common. People hid from each other, camouflaged them-selves, found masks. He said that at one stage he deliberately adopted the mask of being gay, to torment those—teachers and pupils—whom he saw as too stupid to see through it; and to protect his inner self, which school, daily, violated.

He foresaw a problem, however, were classes to be smaller:

I don't know how many teachers would want to expose themselves as human beings, or whether pupils would want to show themselves, or hide themselves away in the back row, get away with doing damn little and just scrape through . . .

It was as if he saw these stratagems as so inevitable a part of life in school, that it was impossible to imagine reform removing their necessity. I share his feeling of the inevitability of schools being like schools being like schools; of the extraordinary nature of schools and the life which goes on in them:

School is in fact one of the most strange places you could ever witness in your life; and it's only a pity that you've got that between the ages of 5 and 15, and you haven't really got to grips with what it is.

I think most people, when they think of what went on in school, they're in hysterics. I honestly believe that school is a totally weird organization.

But he does believe, as I do, that:

I can't help feeling that if this [the closing of the gap in smaller classes. Teachers and pupils being able to behave as human beings] was allowed to happen—I don't know if it's my age, or whatever—it would be okay. I believe that you wouldn't get kids dropping out or just skiving because they can't stand it.

In fact, if teachers did say, look we're human beings, we're just here to help you learn—people wouldn't have to run away from it, because it wouldn't be this big front, of teachers and kids and bullying and discipline and arrogance.

There wouldn't be anything to run away from, because they would be human beings.

Mark, then, is saying that if you were to make classes a great deal smaller, and if you were to remove the 'complete and utter gap', teachers and pupils could behave in a more human way. Teachers would be free to behave as authoritative parents—rather as Mark's history teacher seems to have behaved—and not as panicking warders or purblind diplomats.

It seemed remarkable to me that a boy, fresh from what had been an unenjoyable schooling, should have had the clarity of mind to sense, if not to state directly, that he and his teachers had been victims of circumstances—instead of abandoning them to his bitterness. His question whether it was they or he who began his hostile and 'immature' behaviour, is pregnant with an insight never quite delivered: that relations between him and his teachers were governed not by choices but by constraints.

I must stress before leaving Mark that the sort of human being he wanted as a teacher—Mark, the very epitome of the hostile, rebellious, cynical, flamboyant adolescent—was not a weak sympathetic cipher, but someone strong; someone empowered by favourable circumstances to be strong; to be an authoritative parent.

'There would be nothing to run away from'

This phrase has echoes worth catching. Mark was talking about the possible effect of greater humanity on life in classrooms; the effect of closing the gap. A sum can be done.

Smaller numbers mean:

— Less stress
— Less fear, to force teachers into keeping their distance, and into impercipient generalization, and relegation
— More time for each pupil in a class
— More proximity between teacher and pupil
— More chance of acknowledgement
— More warmth
— More good humour
— More ability to take risks, to prompt active learning, to provoke the retiring
— Less fear of foolish prominence for pupils when they speak.

Whereas larger numbers mean:

— Great stress
— Artificiality; splits, clowns, scapegoats
— Distance between teacher and pupil
— Anxiety and defensiveness: the diplomat or martinet posture
— Relegation of too many
— Urgent dependence on a chosen few for reward and a sense of safety
— Dependence for peace on those relegated to Nomansland
— Covert tuition for the chosen few
— Fear for pupils of looking foolish if they dare to speak.

Larger numbers mean an atmosphere unlikely to be met again later in life; an atmosphere unique to the years between 5 and 18; and for too many, uniquely inimical.

My witnesses from Nomansland were running away from an inhuman predicament forced on teachers and pupils by the size of classes. The attitude of their teachers towards them was neither subtle nor generous nor speculative. Their teachers could be inattentive, inflexible; at worst, both vindictive and patronizing.

What they saw across the 'gap' when they looked at Anne, Paul, David, Jane, Joanne, was blurred, vague, easily misinterpreted—as it is possible to misinterpret things too far away to be seen with accuracy. The 'gap' prevented these teachers from seeing my witnesses clearly.

Class-size research

Claire Burstall, in a very interesting article, reports on class-size research in general; and refers to a large study of French teaching in different sorts of primary schools, carried out by the National Foundation for Educational Research. Small rural schools were observed; as were much larger urban schools.

Significantly more teachers in small classes were described as having a 'positive' attitude toward the children they were teaching than were those in larger classes.

Further, in the small rural schools in the sample, which contained a disproportionate number of classes containing fewer than fifteen pupils, not only were the teachers' attitudes more positive, but so also were those of their pupils. The level of French was also consistently higher than that of the rest of the pupils in the sample, in spite of the fact that from the socio-economic point of view, the small-school pupils were at a relative disadvantage. And certainly from the point of view of the resources available to them the small schools were at a considerable disadvantage.

She goes on to say that these small-class pupils went on to secondary school and maintained their advantage there. She asks herself why. Evidence, she says, suggested:

that closer teacher–pupil relationships might be a factor influencing the development of positive attitudes, and the fostering of a high level of pupil achievement.

These closer relationships—the gap narrowing—seem to have been the result not so much of smaller number itself, but of a greater possibility of warmth and humanity in the rural schools, to which smaller number was the crucial contributor.

We can fairly imagine that teachers and pupils in these smaller classes in rural schools related to each other as parents and children. Teaching always in such schools, their humanity, generosity and empathy were intact. Never having had to deal with crowds, they were less capable of impercipience, relegation, benign or vindictive neglect. It is of the utmost importance to dwell on the fact that most of their teaching experience had been in conditions that did not allow them to suffer from the effects of teaching large classes, and the consequent stress. Their experience had left them powerful.

But the study also observed and interviewed teachers who had known less benign circumstances. Burstall quotes these comments from teachers now working with small classes, but used to much larger ones:

the teacher gets to know the child . . . learns how not to pressure the child but how to make him feel secure and wanted. The teacher uses the good rapport to stimulate learning. Co-operation is much greater and better . . .

I find that I do really know all my kids. When I look back, I suppose I only ever knew twenty or so [an overestimate, I suspect] of my kids in the large classes I have always had. It is such an advantage. You know their problems, likes, dislikes, and can more easily reform attitudes. The children . . . all feel very close to me and all will come to me for help or to talk to confide or just be near . . .

This is an account of teachers freed to feel and act like parents. Most people probably go into teaching with the phantasy or the clear intention of being able to work in such a way with their pupils. Most teachers have generous feelings that they want to put to use. Smaller classes let those feelings flourish.

Burstall also mentions comments typically made by teachers facing classes of thirty to forty pupils:

I am not pleased with the amount of time I have to spend with each child; I find it very frustrating not being able to get around and talk to the children individually as much as I would like.

You do not get to know any child well,

says another teacher.

Those who are shy you rarely talk with . . .

and not talking with them means not getting to know them—so leads to the use of a great, vague, baggy category like 'shy' to put them all into, so that you feel better about their inaccessibility. Relegation, again.

Your main concern is marking, planning and discipline. The pupils themselves become blank faces you are talking at, receptacles you are cramming knowledge, skills, morals into. The few children you do get to know and achieve an understanding with are then considered teachers' pets.

The reason for the ubiquitous use of that phrase, 'teacher's pet', is simple. Classes everywhere are big. Pupils in all big classes are divided into those the teacher acknowledges, and those she does not. The pejorative implication of the phrase stems from the defensive urgency with which teachers are forced to find and keep trusted allies in their crowds. The acknowledged in large classes seem 'pets' because teachers need them so badly.

Teachers' pets: the members of the teacher's 'family': those on whom she lavishes her desire to teach properly; those on whom she lavishes her skill.

CHAPTER ELEVEN

Time to think and discuss

A TEACHER without time to think is like an artist asked to paint without being able to stand back and look at the results of what she's doing. And when, in the end, she sees that her picture is a flop, she blames not her restricted space, her need to work very fast, her inability to stand back and take cogent squints at her latest brush strokes. No, she blames the canvas.

It is no good saying teachers can think after work. After dealing with a succession of crowds of adolescents, a teacher is incapable of detached, dispassionate thought. One crowd succeeds another. So much, and of such complexity, happens with the second crowd, that precise recall of what went on with the first is very difficult. If no time is allocated for reflection and analysis, you will not learn from what may have gone wrong with particular pupils, nor be able to make accurate alterations in your approach to them.

Every lesson taught should, ideally, be followed by time for thought, and—as often as possible—for discussion with other teachers.

A teacher's so-called 'free' time is no use. It is inevitably used for marking, planning, or recuperation from the class war. There is ludicrously little of it, anyway. In all my teaching experience, I never had more than four or five 'free' periods a week, out of a total of thirty-five to forty.

At the Ashby Unit, we talked about every child every day between 9 and 10 o'clock in the morning; and every child would be regularly discussed at the ward round, and at case conferences. Why should the psychiatrically ill be so privileged? All my witnesses would have benefited from discussion about them, by all their teachers, on regular occasions. Each was shelved where thought were not; and thus relegated, no discussion was considered necessary.

Regular discussion would make misjudgement of Nomanslanders less likely; and might even help to lift a misjudgement once powerfully stuck. Discussion opens up categories; prises apart presumptions that sanction inattention. Lack of it is dangerous.

Because they have too little time for co-operation, thought, and discussion, teachers tend to be isolated. Early in your career, you are told that one of the glories of the profession is autonomy: you can shut your door and get on with the job. In fact, autonomy is a grave disadvantage: teachers do not have to refer to each other for verification of their ideas about their pupils. As 'autonomous' professionals, they are made to feel that they have a right to their misjudgements, which can thrive unchallenged. Moreover, the other side of 'autonomy' is private suffering: many teachers in difficulty are burdened by the phantasy that only they are failing. They would know that their difficulties are not unique if teachers regularly watched each other at work, or worked together.

And pupils should enjoy regular conferences. One teacher can trap a pupil in a demeaning misjudgement, which can have disproportionate power to harm. In adolescence in particular, we are probably more prone to be deeply affected by negative than by positive evidence about ourselves.

I now want to exemplify the possible harm of lack of time to think by looking at the predicaments of two pupils.

Margaret

Margaret was a pupil at the comprehensive school at which I carried out much of my research. The statements her teachers made to me about her were extraordinarily varied, adding up to a considerable enigma. Had they talked about Margaret together, some interesting revelations might have occurred, which could have led to change in the way she was judged, and in the expectations of her potential achievement. But each statement was from behind closed doors—was a pronouncement from each teacher's autonomous kingdom to me, a visiting emissary from the Empire of Research. It seemed obvious to me that no comparison had been made between these monarchs' widely differing ideas.

Five of her seven teachers had picked her as someone 'hard to know, biddable, easily overlooked'. She had been placed on entry into the school in the lowest stream—on the basis of tests, and reports from her previous school. She had attended this school for a year only, failing to settle during a time of very great disruption for her family.

One of the oddest details on her records was that although her recorded IQ was low, her reading age on entry to the school was three years ahead of her chronological age. Expectations, when I came to interview her and her teachers, were according to her streaming were:

that she was capable of a few CSEs; but what seemed to be going on in some of her subjects was at variance with this.

Her English teacher told me that Margaret had asked her if she could try English O level instead of CSE. Her teacher dissuaded her—knowing, she said, that Margaret would not be able to cope. But this certainty seemed slightly at variance with her belief that Margaret would get a CSE Grade 2—since a CSE 1 pass is the equivalent of a pass at O level. Contradictory too was this comment:

I find her very organized. She's always got something to do. She reads very widely and makes a sensitive response to whatever she has read.

I thought of David; of the certainty of his school that he was only capable of CSE, and my original belief that he would only pass CSE English. Some years later, he passed English A level with a B.

Her English teacher then said something very interesting, and pregnant with the implication that Margaret may have been keeping her own expectations of herself too low—in collusion with her teachers' relegation:

She does tend to work with others far below her own ability. She works with the less able girls who are inclined to let her do it for them, really.

I wondered what would have happened had she been encouraged to work with more able classmates, or elevated to a higher 'set' altogether. I wondered why her teacher had not thought of this, since she said to me:

I think she still has a lot of potential that has not yet revealed itself fully.

I felt with force that this teacher had not discussed Margaret with herself, let alone with her colleagues.

I guessed that she had not tried to make a connection between, say, her idea of Margaret's untapped potential, and the fact that she tended to work with those less able than herself. An attempt to connect them might have bred this suspicion: Margaret works with the less able because part of her *feels* less able than her more optimistic idea of her ability—reflected in her desire to try for O level—suggests. To have put her with some 'more able' pupils might have been a chance of releasing her 'potential'.

It can safely be assumed that my interview with this teacher offered her the first opportunity she had had to formulate and elaborate her thoughts about Margaret at length. But there was no pressure on her to translate thought and talk into review and adaptation of approach and expectation; to examine an explanation based on the familiar mixture of a firm category accepted (lowest stream), with blurred loose thoughts which don't fit the category.

She produced one by one the components of the girl's paradoxical predicament:

—she couldn't do O level
—she'll get a CSE 2
—she's very organized and reads widely
—she works with others below her ability
—she has a lot of unrevealed potential.

It is as if this teacher's comments are a sequence of precise reflections of some of the facets of the girl's own confusion. She has various ideas of who she is. Her teacher catches these ideas, one by one, and reflects them.

What did her other teachers think? Her art teacher said:

She's very withdrawn. She works hard for me . . . but she's one of those people—

Look at that phrase 'those people' for its implication that the overlooked are numerous: they are 'those people', a group, a legion, a large problem.

—who it is easy to overlook because she is so sort of quiet and mousy. I would say she's reasonably intelligent: two or three good O levels, and the rest good CSEs.

Her maths teacher—offering a notion at variance with his own nomination of her as 'biddable, easy to overlook', suggesting again a lack of thought—said:

She has become distinctly troublesome . . .

What had happened, I wondered. Did his colleagues know of this aberrant change? Her two PE teachers noted her 'independence', and the fact that others did not seem to like her very much. They thought she probably wasn't very bright.

Most interesting of all were her chemistry teacher's comments. She expected her to achieve a CSE Grade 1 pass—the equivalent of a pass at O level. She said that she was surprised that Margaret was in the lowest stream. She was a pupil whom she had started to notice chiefly because of the quality of her written work in a 'low' chemistry set; and also because she eventually began to feel guilty that she had tended to overlook her, as she was so withdrawn. So she began to make a special point of talking to her, of making herself available, one to one, bending over her desk to be asked questions.

She's done every question . . . she's very keen to get on . . .

But she too noticed that Margaret is isolated socially:

I don't feel she's got many friends at all . . .

It was clear from what this teacher said that she saw Margaret as someone of whose potential she no longer had any clear idea; but she was sure it was greater than had been suspected, and than the expectations enshrined in her streaming. This seemed to exemplify the fact that if a relationship is achieved between teacher and pupil, categorization is unlatched; expectations tend to become bolder; possibilities previously masked, are glimpsed; optimism and generosity replace dismissive, pessimistic presumption. Unmistakable, too, was affection in the way this teacher talked about the girl.

I feel that hidden among these varying ideas was the unexpressed possibility that Margaret had been completely misperceived—as completely as David.

Hidden, at least, is a revelation that she *may* have a great deal more to offer than has been suspected. However, not only did her teachers not have occasion to talk to each other about her, but their inattention to her was also guaranteed by her extreme quietness. Only her chemistry teacher had looked closely at her—intrigued by the contrast between Margaret's silence and her work; and guilty about her own neglect. It was her perceptions, above all, that Margaret's other teachers needed to hear.

Margaret interviewed

When I talked to Margaret, I sensed that I was talking to someone whose intelligence was immured behind defences against alarm. I admired her courage for agreeing to talk to me—because she was obviously very ill at ease. A thin girl, she spoke with timid brevity; and seemed, often, not to hear what I had said because she was concentrating so hard on her discomfort. She seemed abashed; someone whose energies were monopolized by anxiety. Her chemistry and PE teachers had told me of times when she had been bullied: when a shoe had been stolen, for instance, and she had been silently miserable, and defenceless against her tormentors. I had a picture of a strange girl, isolated and unhappy. She told me that she hated it when teachers shouted; that she couldn't concentrate when classes were noisy and anarchic; that she liked her chemistry teacher because she was 'friendly', because she talked to her.

It seemed clear that this teacher's acknowledgement had much to do with Margaret's success in chemistry. I felt that she had been deprived of the possibility of similar success—at variance with her streaming—in other subjects; and that inattention and lack of thought were to blame. What, I wondered, would have happened if all her teachers, unanimously, had adopted the approach of Mrs Trench, her chemistry teacher?

Margaret's case suggests that lack of opportunity to think and talk means that dissonant views of a pupil can quite easily exist; but do not collide in discussion to produce insight and change. It suggests that in a misjudged pupil's schooling, there will always be, somewhere, a crucial perception waiting to detonate revelation. But because the autonomous teacher keeps his perception to himself, no explosion takes place. (Even if he makes it available in a report, his fellow monarchs are more likely to record its difference from their own views, and respect his perception, than talk to him about it, or try to learn from it. There's no time for anything else . . .)

Margaret's reticence and camouflage reinforced the improbability of her ever being discussed. All might have been different if, each week, each month, Margaret's teachers had enjoyed opportunity to talk about her, systematically. But there was no time for that. Crowd on crowd on crowd on crowd. Then lethargy in the evening, or some automatous book marking or planning.

Cheryl

At least Margaret's relegation—neglectful and demeaning though it may have been—was not vindictive. But it seemed that Cheryl's teachers had written her off. With occasion to talk about what they were doing, I think they would have been at least very worried, and probably horrified.

In the same year as Margaret, Cheryl—disengaged, uncommunicative—had come to be seen as deliberately uncooperative, deliberately disenchanted. It was as if her teachers wanted to blame her for not giving them more. Her predicament was complex; but it was seen in simple terms, as if all she had to do was to be co-operative again. I guessed that her chief problem was that she had come to see adults as people who offered her little but unhelpful pressure and criticism; and that in their presence she seemed stubborn and sulky and unresponsive.

She came into the interview room diffidently, after a quiet knock. I got up from my seat where I had been fiddling with my tape-recorder, and faced a slim, pretty girl with short dark hair, who smiled provisionally at me, and then looked at the ground. She seemed at once shy, unconfident and not happy. I sensed the sort of unhappiness that acts like a screen between you and life, but you know neither why it is there nor what it is made of. I felt my spirits drop, very slightly.

Her voice was flat. As she answered my questions, she found it hard to look at me. In the course of an interview that lasted about forty minutes, she seemed to be forever saying, 'all right'. The phrase appears sixteen times in the transcript.

Do you like French, I asked her.

It's all right, I like the teacher.

What's all right about the lessons?

Well, the people in the lesson are all right and they don't mess about and the teacher's friendly and everything, she's not that strict . . .

'All right' suggested a depressed survivor's stoicism. She was saying, 'I can't expect very much'.

Her teachers agreed that she did not take an active part in lessons, was not someone who joined in and attracted attention. They seemed to find her presence disturbing, dissatisfying.

Mrs Carr, her French teacher, said:

I've had her for two years and she's rather quiet. She tends to sit there and she doesn't want to draw attention; she always looks rather worried if I do ask her a question. She occasionally asks me things, but as I am going round the class.

If she does ask Cheryl a question:

I feel she doesn't want to answer . . . I don't know Cheryl. I don't think she wants me to know her, so I can't really like her.

She feels rebuffed by Cheryl, and a failure to like is the result.

Cheryl just seems to want to get away from me, and only do the work I force her to do. She's a little bit lazy—she can do it, but she needs to be forced into doing it . . .

It is interesting that Mrs Carr's feelings do not fit Cheryl's—in that Mrs Carr was the only teacher Cheryl said she liked. Her positive feelings about this teacher had evidently not been very well communicated; had not been noticed—had been misjudged.

Perhaps what Cheryl was saying was that Mrs Carr would be a likeable teacher if only they could get to know each other. I felt that Cheryl had become indifferent to school; that she saw possibilities, but could never seize them. She needed to be cleverly lured into contact and activity.

Her drama teacher, Mrs Brown, corroborated my feeling about her:

Cheryl I feel has drifted away, she was much more relaxed last year . . . doesn't smile much, moves beautifully . . . she's very much pressured by home. She's only an average girl—

Note the familiar mixture of certainty and vagueness: someone who is adrift is nevertheless definable as 'only average'.

—but they see her as being a doctor or something, so there's pressure . . .

As well as being confused and constrained by circumstances beyond her control—teaching Cheryl in a class of twenty-six, for instance—Mrs Brown, like Mrs Carr, is intelligent, considerate, sensitive. She notes —but implies that she is helpless to do anything about it, now:

I think the fault is also mine, I think she's become more withdrawn perhaps because I didn't spot it early enough, I didn't see she was beginning to drift . . .
I should have spotted what was happening and tried to speak to her individually in order to reassure her, whereas she's becoming more isolated.

'Adrift' suggests well what has become of a girl whose low feelings about herself have made approval and disapproval, exhortation and criticism, disappointment and irritation—all equally meaningless. Mrs Brown is perhaps more charitable than Mrs Carr in what she feels about Cheryl; but they both used the word 'drift', and both seem only able to note that she is drifting. Their stated helplessness felt almost disinterested, as if Cheryl was no real concern of theirs.

Cheryl's comments about Mrs Brown throw light on the teacher's comments and seem to corroborate them. She talked of others in the class who took part, and said more. Does the teacher spend more time with them, I asked.

Yes. I feel that because they're more friendly towards her . . . yes I think she does.

When does she talk to you, I asked.

Only when it's really necessary . . . with the outgoing girls she's more friendly, as if she knows them, but with me it's just doing her job, kind of thing.

It would be hard to find a more precise formulation of the difference between what it feels like to be acknowledged, and what it feels like to be relegated.

Does that hurt you, I asked.

Not really.

What does it make you feel?

I think sometimes I feel a bit put out, but I know that's probably because I don't speak out, and don't talk with her.

In other words, she blames herself.

School was teaching Cheryl how to behave in such a way as to encourage adults to be unfriendly; school was—I suspect—helping to confirm her low opinion of herself. But how could Mrs Brown, with a crammed timetable and a big class and no time to pause and reflect, do anything about her predicament? Cheryl did not help her. She kept her feelings to herself: she could not explain that she felt left out. Instead, she gained a little more evidence, from her teachers' neglect, that she was the sort of person who *should be* left out: evidence to support a meagre hypothesis of her own worth.

Nor could she approach Mrs Carr and let her know that she liked, or would like to like her. Instead, she kept her distance, and Mrs Carr came to feel negative towards her. More good hard evidence.

There is implicit cruelty in accepting this girl's unhappiness; and cruel presumption in Mrs Carr's claim that Cheryl didn't want to be known. If she had enjoyed a regular chance to analyse her relations with the girl, Mrs Carr would have realized this. But she had no time to focus her sensitivity and generosity on Cheryl—and was forced to let the girl be a victim of her disgruntlement.

Teachers expressed their views with doubt, suggesting again that they had not had opportunity to think out their ideas about Cheryl.

Mrs Carr said:

I *suspect* Cheryl lacks confidence.

Mr Thraill, her biology teacher, said:

I don't think she's really got the intelligence to make it on her own; and she's one I ought to help if I had more time . . . she doesn't pay enough attention.

Her chemistry teacher, Mrs Trench, who awarded such generosity to Margaret, felt far more rebuffed than Mrs Carr. She too expressed uncertainty; but a definite dislike as well:

I've gone off her. I feel she's drifted away from me—

Here, I feel, we have the strange idea of deliberate, intentional drifting.

—she doesn't say much, but she mutters under her breath about me [how did she know the girl was talking about her if she was muttering?]. She's drifting away from me, and that's a shame—I don't think she likes the discipline. I feel she's a bit slippery, deceptive, elusive.

Rebuffed, she uses pejorative words like 'slippery'; but note the uncertainty of 'I don't think . . .' and 'I feel'. Her guesses are hurried, made in the warmth of her disappointment. She looks at the sulky face that presents Cheryl's demoralization, and 'goes off' her. She sees her muttering, and assumes it's about her. She snatches a word, 'slippery', with which to relegate her and adjust her self-respect: knowing she is an excellent teacher, she must explain her failure to reach Cheryl.

To consider what she is doing to Cheryl, to appreciate the vindictiveness of her dismissal of the girl, Mrs Trench needed to talk to other teachers—and, of course, to talk to Cheryl herself. She needed, above all, set times to think about the girl. Instead, teacher and pupil stay well apart, separated by a jungle of incompatible and unjustifiable hypotheses about each other.

I watched Cheryl being taught by Mrs Trench. She listened to not a word her teacher said, and gossiped quietly to her neighbour throughout the lesson—her neighbour, in turn, apparently taking no notice of what Cheryl was saying. It seemed saddest of all that she should be beyond the range of a teacher I rated as gifted and generous; and I had the impression that she was isolated from her peers as well.

She's always got a blank face . . .

Said her PE teacher.

I picked her up four times in one day, for minor things—things that show you a
kid who's not in the path they're supposed to go on—for no apparent reason—

said the deputy head teacher, responsible for discipline. Perhaps if she
and her colleagues had talked about Cheryl, that reason would have
materialized.

Her English teacher saw things they could usefully have discussed. He
sensed:

some sort of discontinuity between the way she is and her potential . . . but she
is just sort of quiet and biddable and not very assertive. Very nice.

His 'but' says much: being quiet and biddable, she did not force that
discontinuity to be examined. And in discussion, his 'very nice' might
have collided usefully with Mrs Trench's 'I've gone off her.' He
also said:

I think Cheryl could do a bit better actually . . . there's hidden things to
Cheryl.

She would not disclose them; her teachers needed to co-operate and
think to find them.

Cheryl needed her teachers' help. Interesting was Mrs Brown's suggestion that her parents wanted her to 'be a doctor or something'.
Perhaps she was someone for whom expectations, from one quarter at
least, were too high; and who, beneath their pressure, could only fail and
become depressed.

What fascinates me most about Cheryl is that her teachers did not
suggest that they wanted to know more about her, or try to decipher the
confusion of their own feelings. Yes, her English teacher talked of
'hidden potential'; but it was if he were quite content that her promise
should be hidden; as if 'hidden potential' was a recognized part of school
life, to be expected from time to time and not to be interfered with. I felt
that the phrase was for him just another category to secure his inattention; a relegation device to let him say, what can I do until she stops
hiding and begins to show herself to me?

In part, their lack of concern to find out more about the girl expresses
their helplessness. It was sensibly protective not to be too concerned,
to let explanation go no further than itself. They have doubts about
Cheryl, which they express cogently enough; but doubt never leads to
action with a pupil so well relegated.

Nevertheless, the ruthlessness of some of the things they say in relegating her is remarkable. It is a reflection of their need to explain failure in ways least calculated to threaten their security and self-esteem. Immaturity and resistance to authority are quite sinful enough to justify neglect; but slyness, such as they attribute to Cheryl, is a much better ground for relegation. Why should Mrs Trench waste her limited time on a slippery girl?

Cheryl certainly is failing, and failing grievously. Forced to explain this, one teacher is nonchalantly inattentive, and talks of hidden potential; but Mrs Trench and Mrs Carr snatch their most negative feelings about the girl and flourish them as adequate explanation. 'I don't think she wants me to know her, so I can't like her'; 'I've gone off her'; '. . . adrift in drama, and there's really nothing I can do to get her back to shore again.'

Mrs Carr's and Mrs Trench's reactions are relegation at its purest, its most cruel, and its most suggestive of teachers' helplessness. They were both warm, humane people. But with lack of time to examine their feelings and their relations with their pupils, and with too many of them to teach, they cannot be warm and humane to all. They were helpless to forestall or neutralize the negative feelings they unavoidably developed for this unresponsive girl.

The danger is that negative feelings, unexamined, never discussed, become aids to swift relegation. This is what I mean by Cheryl's teachers' using their hostility as explanation: Mrs Carr used her resentment at being rebuffed as the route to her conclusion about the girl. There were two stages to this process: (1) she doesn't respond to me; (2) I don't think she wants me to know her. To get from (1) to (2), Mrs Carr mounts her resentment.

Discussion would have shown her this, would have made clear that her relations with Cheryl, and her tendency to give her not much attention, were governed by resentment.

Reflection by her teachers was the only chance this girl possessed of just consideration. She did not know how to demand their thought and time; they did not realize what they were doing to her.

Had Cheryl's teachers talked about her, they would have realized what they were doing, and would probably, as I say, have been horrified. They would have appreciated the possibility that Cheryl's predicament was complex and worthy of examination; would have tried to piece together what evidence they had about her; and, finally, they would have tried to decide a way of altering their approach.

Unanimously. Teachers' most potent weapon is unanimity. The opportunity to discuss your pupils is, above all, a chance to decide on a joint approach; to abandon spurious autonomy. More time to think would allow teachers to escape their isolation, and to enjoy co-operation; and their pupils—particularly those abandoned to Nomansland—would benefit greatly.

The constraints that deplete and impoverish teachers make them react to their pupils compulsively, defensively, or inattentively. With compulsive generosity and affection, they attend to the members of their 'families'; defensively, they outwit or counter-attack their enemies; inattentively, breathing sighs of relief, they neglect those whose reticent, biddable demeanour makes it safe to relegate them.

Smaller classes and more time to think would give teachers the power to work consciously and intelligently.

More implications of lack of time to think

All my witnesses—and not just Margaret and Cheryl, whose stories, I hope, highlight the issue—suffered from their teachers' lack of time for reflection. In quoting what those teachers said, I have pointed to the absurdity and ruthlessness of their hurried thinking. I have also shown my own absurdity as a teacher: relegating those who rebuffed me; jumping all too nimbly to reassuring conclusions. Circumstances forced us to partial blindness; forced us to divide our charges into those who would benefit from our gifts, and those whose defeats would be honoured by our indifference.

Similar decisions were made—who was to be left, who to be cut and patched—at Scutari. Field medicine is now more effective; is not recognizably the same activity as it was in the Crimean War. But our secondary schools now are *not different enough* from the first state schools of a few decades later.

When I see photographs of huge classes faced by moustached and suited men—in elementary schools in the early years of this century—I recognize too much. And if I could pursue those men through their crammed and urgent days, I would certainly recognize that their employment included neither the obligation nor the opportunity to think deeply and regularly about each one of their pupils.

Working at the Ashby Unit was exciting, because thinking was given the same importance as doing. As a result we worked consciously rather than compulsively; we felt powerful rather than almost out of control—running to try to catch up. And I think we were proudest—all of us, nurses, teachers, doctors, social workers, psychologists—of our joint intelligence.

It is only working in absurd conditions that stupefies teachers. Liberated by smaller numbers of pupils and time for reflection and co-operation, they would perform much more effectively.

In conclusion

IT is perhaps appropriate that I should have ended with an account of Cheryl's schooling; for of all my witnesses, hers seems to me to have been the cruellest dilemma. She was perhaps the most isolated of them all; the most cut off from her teachers' sensitivity and intelligence; and very much the victim of hurried unreflective assumptions.

The fate of those relegated to Nomansland is a reflection of the urgency, the relentless pressure, of life in secondary schools. I have argued in my last chapter for the absolute necessity of time for dispassionate analysis of what you have been doing as a teacher, and as soon after you have done it as possible. Without such time, a teacher is like an officer on a confused battlefield. All his decisions are quick and urgent. Once he has made one and carried it out, he cannot review it instantly, because more decisions have to be made; he cannot give dispassionate attention to all that is happening around him. Those in Nomansland—whether vaguely disliked, or vaguely appreciated, or generating no feelings at all—are his docile, biddable infantry, about whom he has no need to think, because they are always there.

Meanwhile he is free to deal with the mutinous, and bring off tactical successes with his hussars and his lancers: the acknowledged few.

It is impossible to grow intellectually and imaginatively if you are not open to the influence of events and other people. The plight of those in Nomansland is that they are not open, not vulnerable. With their passivity, their inscrutability, their unresponsiveness, their boredom—they build security. Their security is effective defence, and means foreclosure of alternatives, the refusal of risk, the careful accretion of layers of armour against surprise.

Safe, they cannot grow. They can acquire information; but they cannot make what they learn part of their own lives. They can have no mental life at all, if by mental life is meant risky, curious receptiveness to the world around you.

Just as architecture must obey human needs, so should the circumstances in which we expect education to take place be designed to be 'human'. The case I have tried to build against large classes is that they are 'inhuman', in the same way as a tower block of flats can be inhuman. Large classes function. They guarantee an activity, for an economically large number, that may be called—without too much inaccuracy —education. Just so does a tower block work: what it contains can be called—with the same claim to honesty—'homes' or 'life'. But in the large classes of the large schools that flock to my mind as I write, too many pupils are forced defensively into an imitation, a pretence, of education. They write on paper and sit at desks; but what they write is without meaning *for themselves*: without joy, intention, curiosity; so their presence is a sort of absence.

Certainly, many such schools contain great teaching, successful partial conquest of difficult conditions. Many are imaginatively run; and many teachers subvert their circumstances and give their pupils much. But I can't help thinking of the drabness of the schooling of some of those whose stories I have told—of Jane's departure from school, for instance. She had learnt not to expect too much; that she mustn't imagine that the intellectual pleasure she had known as a child would return. So she left school, politely and pleasantly, carrying, instead of a fat sheaf of credentials, a drab defeat certified by her teachers as a sensible choice.

I think of Joanne's belittlement as 'happy to be a bank girl'. While at school, her teachers seemed to like her: she gave them no trouble. But their smiles were smiles of convenience. Once she became an office worker, she may have experienced what happened to a friend of mine then working as a secretary. A male colleague burst into the room where she was working on her own. He looked around, and said: 'Oh sorry, no one there,' and left.

School had taught Joanne that she was no one. Such pupils fail to experience excitement and risk. Life becomes known too soon. But education should encourage a sense of life's unpredictability; should perpetuate a small child's voracious curiosity.

What David and Anne experienced for the first time when they broke the drab contracts their schools had sealed for them, was the pleasure of dangerous participation; of not being daunted by the number and variety of possible interpretations, ideas, opinions. To be 'educated' means to enjoy possibility; to take on the inconceivable; to be perplexed by confusion, like one of Socrates' victims—but to endure it, for the pleasure of clarity which does sometimes arrive.

To continue education in adolescence and beyond, you must go on having the confidence to interrogate the world and the people in it. For those who end up in Nomansland, interrogation is over.

I watched a TV programme recently about genetics. Four scientists talked at length. All had gone through endless hours of automatous grind: they were no strangers to 'stuffing'. But they were all lit up by curiosity; and what they talked of most was not their knowledge but their ignorance. Everything they said seemed to lead to what they did not know and wanted to know. The ingenuity of their hunt for answers was wonderful; and, like all scientists who talk well, they made me sense the complexity of what lies behind the 'reality' I take for granted.

They were full of a pioneering pleasure that made them seem like absorbed children. Their eyes shone as they talked. Their gestures were fluent. Words did their bidding, promptly and lucidly. Sometimes they said things that sounded naïvely baffled. One confessed that though he was beginning to understand how limbs are genetically planned, he will for ever find it astonishing that a person's arms end up the same length.

If education atrophies the capacity for naïve bafflement, for astonishment, it is no education at all. For too many pupils in secondary school —and for all in Nomansland—the possibility of being astonished by their own arms has come to an end.

Intellectual pleasure is not the preserve of the intellectually gifted. In my experience, it has sometimes been the most backward who have successfully kept a young child's intellectual gleefulness. It has been their luck—perhaps—to avoid the often deadening effects of the hunt for credentials; just as the acknowledged few are lucky, that their confidence and attractiveness win them the sort of teaching that transcends 'stuffing'.

Lucky, too, are those like David, Anne and Paul, who have escaped their schools' effect on them. But it is only smaller classes and more time for teachers to think that will make it unnecessary for pupils to rely on luck to gain a proper education.

Possible measures now

Such changes will be expensive, but, without going into a great deal of detail, I would like to suggest what could be done now—particularly about the plight of those in Nomansland.

1. Training to recognize evasion

The silence and evasiveness of some pupils should be recognized by teachers as possibly suspicious. Training needs to be so devised that teachers are made aware of the power of adolescents to dissemble, and of the fact that what their pupils show of themselves is not necessarily a good guide to what they are.

Such a training in complexity would succeed best if student teachers were put into apprenticeship to selected teachers whose work they could watch, groups from whose classes they could teach, and by whom they themselves could be watched and enlightened. During such an apprenticeship, the expectation would be that trainer and learner would continually discuss their differing views of pupils; and out of such discussion would develop an awareness of the difficulty of definitive judgement.

This sort of practice is already being introduced in training courses. But during teacher training as I have known it, as perpetrator and consumer, there is too little scope for the careful consideration of particular pupils. The postgraduate variety that I know best is still an assault course for the trainee; an abrupt initiation into too many terrors and a few intoxicating rewards.

Instead, students should be given the smallest possible number of pupils to teach *at first*—taking groups out of their trainers' classes. Awareness of pupils as individuals would then have a chance to grow before development of the ability to manage crowds. At present trainees may be given crowds straight away; and may be driven too soon into a defensive rigidity of judgement and explanation; shoring up their safety with as much certainty about their pupils as possible.

Such a training would mean that probation would become active co-operation between trainer and trainee—as it certainly is in some schools—rather than a time of assessed, but solitary, initiation.

2. Training pupils to talk

One simple and cheap practical change would be the recognition that talk and discussion are not just advantageous, but indispensable for intellectual growth. GCSE begins to do this.

Every school allocates time for 'pastoral' work. A class teacher and her class meet once a day for twenty minutes or half an hour. In some schools their time together is used to great effect; in others—I suspect most—it is used for the handing-out of necessary information, and for private business with 'problem' children. It has been my experience that pastoral care exists primarily for such pupils—because of the trouble they cause to all. So, rather than guiding all sheep, the pastoral teacher—with too little time to do anything else—guides strays.

Some redefinition of straying would help. It should be accepted that pupils who are nicely quiet might be intellectual strays. This acceptance could only come from consent in the importance of talk in learning; so that the silent would be seen as possibly at a loss.

Pastoral time could then be used, among other things, to train pupils to talk. To carry out such work—of the sort I have described being done at the Ashby Unit—a group needs to be small. But this could be arranged.

Think of a 'year' of 200 pupils. On Monday and Wednesday, the seven pastoral classes into which the year is divided themselves divide into two groups of thirteen to fifteen. One becomes a 'study-skills' group; the other becomes part of a crowd—at assembly, or watching an educational film, or listening to a visiting speaker. On Tuesday and Thursday, the crowd subdivides into training groups.

Here is not the place for detail about what the groups would do. It is enough to say that their work would allow those in Nomansland to try out a different demeanour. 'Nobody taught me *how* to ask a question . . .' said Jane. To learn how to talk in class, she needed such training.

3. Number

Stuffing may be a necessity, forced on teachers by the difficulty and stress of managing crowds. It is possible, too, that—with constraints unaltered, circumstances unimproved—the new obligation to carry out a great deal of assessment may increase the pressure on teachers to relegate numbers of their pupils. An open mind is time consuming. The more responsibilities teachers take on, the greater the pressure to make glib, ruthless judgements of their pupils.

But there is a more optimistic case to be made about these matters. If, for instance, more active, talkative learning is too difficult in crowds for teachers to promote it regularly rather than occasionally, they and parents may come to demand the smaller numbers that make it possible. What university teacher, acknowledging the importance of discussion, would accept thirty-two students in a seminar?

But number, in the sort of way I have suggested in my sketch of how 'pastoral' time could be better used—could be handled more flexibly in schools.

There are occasions when it is right to put pupils in large numbers, thus releasing some teachers to work with much smaller numbers. The occasions may be few; but they should be used. In one comprehensive I know, experiment of this kind had been carried out with fifth- and sixth-year classes. It was decided that in certain subjects, lessons could be divided into lectures and seminars: the former appropriate for large numbers, the latter for small.

4. Auxiliary help

As in many other things, primary schools have led in the use of parents and others as auxiliaries. Bringing people from outside to work in schools is healthy anyway; and the judicious use of auxiliaries—whether volunteers, or part-time and paid—could release teachers to work with smaller groups. One teacher 'team teaching' with one auxiliary halves the number for which he alone is responsible.

5. Auxiliary as advocate

If it is agreed that talking about all pupils regularly is important, in order to avoid making mistakes of judgement about them, then a system could be organized to give needy pupils a teacher or auxiliary as advocate. The most elusive pupils would be seen as most in need of an advocate—whose responsibility would be to argue, at set times, the most optimistic case for his client against all negative evidence, and against all attempts to trap his client in demeaning misjudgement. In school, pessimistic cases often—mysteriously—seem easier to carry than optimistic ones. An effect of stress and impossible conditions is a seepage of pessimism into teachers' thoughts about their pupils. It can be difficult to argue optimistically for a pupil in a climate of pessimism. A system of formalized advocacy would militate against relegation, against invisibility.

Thorough change

However, change more radical than any reform so far suggested may be necessary.

My travels in Nomansland have taught me that talents and intelligence can become sulky, evasive, anorexic; deliberately refusing nourishment for the most enigmatic of reasons. At least with true anorexia you can assess height and skeleton and say, 'There should be more flesh on this person.' But if intelligence goes into recession, if it is starved or starves itself, it leaves neither skeleton nor stature to remind of its potential amplitude.

Teachers need the humility to admit that knowing a child or adolescent is difficult and takes time; and that judgements and prophecies should be made with great caution, and on the understanding that they may well be wrong.

The best guarantee of intellectual growth for adolescent pupils in schools is acknowledgement by adults imbued with this humility. Other things are necessary too—good equipment, good examinations, books, computers. But relationships must come first. It is only in a 'parental' relationship with a good teacher that an intellectual anorexic can be identified and fed. But this book suggests that, in schools as they now are, acknowledgement will always be selective. Schools, then, must become very different places. There must be more adults in schools; and many of them should be professional teachers. But I have already said that I believe that lay people should be used more in schools. I'm not alone in this belief—in thinking that state education should draw far more freely on the experience and learning of those who live in the communities schools serve. The teacher's job would undergo an interesting and probably gratifying change, if to the duty to teach were to be added the need to train and supervise—for instance—part-time paid, or retired, or student helpers.

I am not advocating an influx into schools of vocational trainers whose chief interest is early recruitment to the work-place and not education at all. I am talking about the assumption, or resumption, by communities of some of the responsibility to educate, which is at present wholly discharged by the teaching profession.

Teachers would be freed by the assistance of other adults. They would be freed most of all from the stress of crowd management, because they would seldom be responsible alone for absurd numbers of pupils. Working co-operatively, teachers' helpers—qualified by their own education to do so—would tutor single pupils or groups of pupils. They would take on specified tasks; someone qualified in Physics supervising a group doing a practical, for example. *Helpers would be at teachers' disposal.*

I do not believe that the difficulties of codifying boundaries and expectations for the work of such helpers would be insuperable. In a recent job at a psychiatric hospital, I had to recruit, train, and supervise volunteers for work of various kinds to do with mental health. The experience taught me that another surmountable difficulty would be that of ensuring that only those with acceptable motives were offered work as helpers.

But the chief lesson of this recent experience was that *auxiliaries liberate professionals*. Rather than taking work away from professionals, helpers share their work and enhance its quality. If anything, they create more work—of a kind. The arrival of helpers in secondary schools would in itself prompt the need for more teachers rather than fewer because of the creation of a new duty to train and supervise.

One crucial advantage of the sort of change I have outlined would be the slackening of the pressures that force misapprehension and misjudgement of their pupils by their teachers. But the greatest benefit of the redistribution of the duty to educate adolescents, would be that pupils would have a much greater chance than exists at present of being acknowledged by one or more of the adults responsible for their education.

A woman I know, now in her early twenties, aptly sums up the dilemma. Without radical change, relegation like hers will continue to be commonplace:

middle people like me, this teacher thought—they're not going to get an A, but they are going to get a C so I can leave them to get on with it.

But she says of her teachers that:

I needed them to say, 'Come on, I know you can do it'—for them to believe that I could do it, really. Because I can't work for myself. I have to have somebody who will know that I am intelligent, and will give me encouragement and coaxing—well, not coaxing, just knowing that I can do the work, that I could get an A for it.

Most pupils need such parental faith from their teachers. None really wants to be invisible.

Suggestions for further reading

ALTHOUGH this book is not academic, it is informed by some wide reading of academic works on education. However, there was a gap of about two years between my main bout of reading, and beginning to write—by which time I knew I was being affected by what I had read, but influences had become indistinct. Books had found shelves in my mind; but I had no catalogue. So it is difficult to do more than acknowledge works to which I make direct reference, and to offer my enthusiasm for some others, which would certainly interest anyone keen to try a choice yard or two of the interminable literature of education.

My book suggests that academic ability is socially influenced, and can be socially stifled. Sociology of education has much to say about this sort of proposition. Read all of David Hargreaves's books. I recommend in particular one written with S. K. Hester and F. J. Mellor:

Deviance in Classrooms RKP, 1975

and another which is not sociology, but recommendation for change:

The Challenge for the Comprehensive School RKP, 1982.

This second book shows that Hargreaves is one of the champions of all who would like imaginative improvements in our system of schooling, rather than regression and mad centralization.

Peter Woods's work I would also suggest to anyone interested in the social dimensions of life in schools:

The Divided School RKP, 1979

Pupil Strategies (edited by Peter Woods) Croom Helm, 1980.

Sociology of education since the late sixties—amplifying earlier work—has an achievement to celebrate: it has examined the minutiae of school life to disclose bit by bit the often deceptive processes which help some to succeed and others to fail. Schools are more understandable as a result. Attitudes in schools are more understandable too, as is the way certain ideas are applied, and the distortion of those ideas by constraints. For a brilliant account of the inimical power of certain constraints on teachers, read:

Sharp, R. and Green, A. *Education and Social Control* RKP, 1975.

For the importance of talk, read Douglas Barnes; and if this is a route you want to follow, his citations will provide you with a map. I would suggest:

Communication to Curriculum Penguin, 1976.

I owe a direct debt to Barnes for his emphasis on the importance of hesitation in thinking. His work must amount to one of the most crucial contributions to thought about education since the war.

I have also referred to, and enthusiastically suggest:

Abercrombie, M. J. *The Anatomy of Judgement* Pelican, 1969.

I have also made reference to the following:

Hudson, Liam *Frames of Mind* Pelican, 1970

Burstall, Claire, 'Time to Mend the Nets'—a Commentary on the Outcomes of Class-Size Research', in *Trends in Education*, no. 3, 1979

Spooner, R. 'Why Small Classes Aren't the Only Answer', in *Education*, no. 22, 1 June 1979. (He suggests, however, that small classes are one of the answers!)

Stanworth, Michelle *Gender and Schooling*—a study of sexual divisions in the classroom. Hutchinson in association with the Explorations in Feminism Collective, 1983

Wilby, Peter 'The Teenage Teachers', in *Sunday Times*, 5 December 1982.

I should also like to mention:

Adams, R. S. and Biddle, B. J. *Realities of Teaching* Holt, 1979. I read this book two years after devising with my colleagues the idea of the 'teaching bottle'. These American scholars had proposed this idea long before, though I did not know it. Their book contains many other fascinating conclusions from their video-recordings of life in classrooms.

Last, but not least, I should like to suggest the books of John Holt, and in particular:

How Children Fail Pelican, 1969.

Index of characters

Index